FICTION Atkinson

Greyfriars Bobby

GREYFRIARS BOBBY

GREYFRIARS
BOBBY

BY
ELEANOR ATKINSON

HARPER & ROW, PUBLISHERS
New York and Evanston

TO
MY HUSBAND

GREYFRIARS BOBBY

WHEN the time-gun boomed from Edinburgh Castle, Bobby gave a startled yelp. He was only a little country dog—the very youngest and smallest and shaggiest of Skye terriers—bred on a heathery slope of the Pentland hills, where the loudest sound was the bark of a collie or the tinkle of a sheep-bell. That morning he had come to the weekly market with Auld Jock, a farm laborer, and the Grassmarket of the Scottish capital lay in the narrow valley at the southern base of Castle Crag. Two hundred feet above it the time-gun was mounted in the half-moon battery on an overhanging, crescent-shaped ledge of rock. In any part of the city the report of the one-o'clock gun was sufficiently alarming, but in the Grassmarket it was an earth-rending explosion directly overhead. It needed to be heard but once there to be registered on even a little dog's brain. Bobby had heard it many times, and he never failed to yelp a sharp protest at the outrage to his ears; but, as the gunshot was always followed by a certain happy event, it started in his active little mind a train of pleasant associations.

In Bobby's day of youth, and that was in 1858, when Queen Victoria was a happy wife and mother, with all her bairns about her knees in Windsor or Balmoral, the Grassmarket of Edinburgh was still a bit of the Middle Ages, as picturesquely decaying and Gothic as German Nuremberg. Beside the classic corn exchange, it had no modern buildings. North and south, along its greatest length, the sunken quadrangle was faced by tall, old, timber-fronted houses of stone, plastered like swallows' nests to the rocky slopes behind them.

Across the eastern end, where the valley suddenly narrowed to the ravine-like street of the Cowgate, the market was spanned by the lofty, crowded arches of George IV. Bridge. This high-hung, viaduct thoroughfare, that carried a double line of buildings within its parapets, leaped the gorge, from the tall, old, Gothic rookeries on High Street ridge, just below the Castle esplanade. It cleared the roofs of the tallest, oldest houses that swarmed up the steep banks from the Cowgate, and ran on, by easy

descent, to the main gateway of Greyfriars kirk‹
yard at the lower top of the southern rise.

Greyfriars' two kirks formed together, under
one continuous roof, a long, low, buttressed build‹
ing without tower or spire. The new kirk was of
Queen Anne's day, but the old kirk was built
before ever the Pilgrims set sail for America. It
had been but one of several sacred buildings, set
in a monastery garden that sloped pleasantly to
the open valley of the Grassmarket, and looked
up the Castle heights unhindered. In Bobby's
day this garden had shrunk to a long, narrow,
high-piled burying-ground, that extended from
the rear of the line of buildings that fronted on
the market, up the slope, across the hilltop, and
to where the land began to fall away again, down
the Burghmuir. From the Grassmarket, kirk
and kirkyard lay hidden behind and above
the crumbling grandeur of noble halls and
mansions that had fallen to the grimiest tenements of Edinburgh's slums. From the end of
the bridge-approach there was a glimpse of massive walls, of pointed windows, and of monumental tombs through a double-leafed gate of
wrought iron, that was alcoved and wedged in
between the ancient guildhall of the candlemakers and a row of prosperous little shops in
Greyfriars Place.

GREYFRIARS BOBBY

A rock-rimmed quarry pit, in the very heart of Old Edinburgh, the Grassmarket was a place of historic echoes. The yelp of a little dog there would scarce seem worthy of record. More in harmony with its stirring history was the report of the time-gun. At one o'clock every day there was a puff of smoke high up in the blue or gray or squally sky, then a deafening crash and a back-fire fusillade of echoes. The oldest frequenter of the market never got used to it. On Wednesday, as the shot broke across the babel of shrill bargaining, every man in the place jumped, and not one was quicker of recovery than wee Bobby. Instantly ashamed, as an intelligent little dog who knew the import of the gun should be, Bobby denied his alarm in a tiny pink yawn of boredom. Then he went briskly about his urgent business of finding Auld Jock.

The market was closed. In five minutes the great open space was as empty of living men as Greyfriars kirkyard on a week-day. Drovers and hostlers disappeared at once into the cheap and noisy entertainment of the White Hart Inn that fronted the market and set its squalid back against Castle Rock. Farmers rapidly deserted it for the clean country. Dwellers in the tenements darted up wynds and blind closes, climbed twisting turnpike stairs to windy roosts under the gables, or they scuttled through noble doors into foul courts and hallways. Beggars and pick-pockets swarmed under the arches of the bridge, to swell the evil-smelling human river that flowed at the dark and slimy bottom of the Cowgate.

A chill November wind tore at the creaking iron cross of the Knights of St. John, on the highest gable of the Temple tenements, that turned its decaying back on the kirkyard of the Greyfriars. Low clouds were tangled and torn on the Castle battlements. A few horses stood about, munching oats from feed-boxes. Flocks of sparrows fluttered down from timbered galleries and rocky ledges to feast on scattered grain. Swallows wheeled in wide, descending spirals from mud villages under the cornices to catch flies. Rats scurried out of holes and gleaned in the deserted corn exchange. And 'round and 'round the empty market-place raced the frantic little terrier in search of Auld Jock.

Bobby knew, as well as any man, that it was the dinner-hour. With the time-gun it was Auld Jock's custom to go up to a snug little restaurant that was patronized chiefly by the decent poor— small shopkeepers, clerks, tenant farmers, and medical students living in cheap lodgings—in Greyfriars Place. There, in Ye Olde Greyfriars

Dining-Rooms, owned by Mr. John Traill, and four doors beyond the kirkyard gate, was a cozy little inglenook that Auld Jock and Bobby had come to look upon as their own. At its back, above a recessed oaken settle and a table, a tiny-paned window looked up and over a retaining wall into the ancient place of the dead.

The view of the heaped-up and crowded mounds and thickets of old slabs and through-stones, girt all about by time-stained monuments and vaults, and shut in on the north and east by the backs of shops and lofty slum tenements, could not be said to be cheerful. It suited Auld Jock, however, for what mind he had was of a melancholy turn. From his place on the floor, between his master's hob-nailed boots, Bobby could not see the kirkyard, but it would not, in any case, have depressed his spirits. He did not know the face of death and, a merry little ruf-fian of a terrier, he was ready for any adventure

On the stone gate pillar was a notice in plain English that no dogs were permitted in Grey-friars. As well as if he could read, Bobby knew that the kirkyard was forbidden ground. He had learned that by bitter experience. Once, when the little wicket gate that held the two tall leaves ajar by day, chanced to be open, he had joyously chased a cat across the graves and over the western wall onto the broad green lawn of Heriot's Hospital.

There the little dog's escapade bred other mischief, for Heriot's Hospital was not a hospital at all, in the modern English sense of being a refuge for the sick. Built and christened in a day when a Stuart king reigned in Holyrood Palace, and French was spoken in the Scottish court, Heriot's was a splendid pile of a charity school, all towers and battlements, and cheerful color, and countless beautiful windows. Endowed by a beruffed and doubleted goldsmith, "Jinglin' Geordie" Heriot, who had "nae braw laddie o' his ain," it was devoted to the care and education of "puir orphan an' faderless boys." There it had stood for more than two centuries, in a spacious park, like the country-seat of a Lowland laird, but hemmed in by sordid markets and swarming slums. The region round about furnished an unfailing supply of "puir orphan an' faderless boys" who were as light-hearted and irresponsible as Bobby.

Hundreds of the Heriot laddies were out in the noon recess, playing cricket and leap-frog, when Bobby chased that unlucky cat over the kirkyard wall. He could go no farther himself, but the laddies took up the pursuit, yelling like Highland clans of old in a foray across the border.

The unholy din disturbed the sacred peace of the kirkyard. Bobby dashed back, barking furiously, in pure exuberance of spirits. He tumbled gaily over grassy hummocks, frisked saucily around terrifying old mausoleums, wriggled under the most enticing of low-set table tombs and sprawled, exhausted, but still happy and noisy, at Auld Jock's feet.

It was a scandalous thing to happen in any kirkyard! The angry caretaker was instantly out of his little stone lodge by the gate and taking Auld Jock sharply to task for Bobby's misbehavior. The pious old shepherd, shocked himself and publicly disgraced, stood, bonnet in hand, humbly apologetic. Seeing that his master was getting the worst of it, Bobby rushed into the fray, an animated little muff of pluck and fury, and nipped the caretaker's shins. There was a howl of pain, and a "maist michty" word that made the ancient tombs stand aghast. Master and dog were hustled outside the gate and into a rabble of jeering slum gamins.

What a to-do about a miserable cat! To Bobby there was no logic at all in the denouement to this swift, exciting drama. But he understood Auld Jock's shame and displeasure perfectly. Good-tempered as he was gay and clever, the little dog took his punishment meekly, and he

8

remembered it. Thereafter, he passed the kirk yard gate decorously. If he saw a cat that needed harrying he merely licked his little red chops—the outward sign of a desperate self-control. And, a true sport, he bore no malice toward the caretaker.

During that first summer of his life Bobby learned many things. He learned that he might chase rabbits, squirrels and moor-fowl, and sea-gulls and whaups that came up to feed in plowed fields. Rats and mice around byre and dairy were legitimate prey; but he learned that he must not annoy sheep and sheep-dogs, nor cattle, horses and chickens. And he discovered that, unless he hung close to Auld Jock's heels, his freedom was in danger from a wee lassie who adored him. He was no lady's lap-dog. From the bairnie's soft cosseting he aye fled to Auld Jock and the rough hospitality of the sheep-fold. Being exact opposites in temperaments, but alike in tastes, Bobby and Auld Jock were inseparable. In the quiet corner of Mr. Traill's crowded dining-room they spent the one idle hour of the week together, happily. Bobby had the leavings of a herring or haddie, for a rough little Skye will eat anything from smoked fish to moor-fowl eggs, and he had the tidbit of a farthing bone to worry at his leisure. Auld Jock smoked tis cutty pipe, gazed at the fire or into the kirk-yard, and meditated on nothing in particular.

In some strange way that no dog could under-stand, Bobby had been separated from Auld Jock that November morning. The tenant of Cauldbrae farm had driven the cart in, himself, and that was unusual. Immediately he had driven out again, leaving Auld Jock behind, and that was quite outside Bobby's brief experience of life. Beguiled to the lofty and coveted driver's seat where, with lolling tongue, he could view this interesting world between the horse's ears, Bobby had been spirited out of the city and carried all the way down and up to the hill-top toll-bar of Fairmilehead. It could not occur to his loyal little heart that this treachery was planned nor, stanch little democrat that he was, that the farmer was really his owner, and that he could not follow a humbler master of his own choosing. He might have been carried to the distant farm, and shut safely in the byre with the cows for the night, but for an incautious remark of the farmer. With the first scent of the native heather the horse quickened his pace, and, at sight of the purple slopes of the Pentlands looming homeward, a fond thought at the back of the man's mind very naturally took shape in speech.

GREYFRIARS BOBBY

·Eh, Bobby, the wee lassie wull be at the tap
o' the brae to race ye hame."

Bobby pricked his drop ears. Within a narrow
limit, and concerning familiar things, the understanding of human speech by these intelligent
little terriers is very truly remarkable. At mention of the wee lassie he looked behind for his
rough old friend and unfailing refuge. Auld
Jock's absence discovered, Bobby promptly
dropped from the seat of honor and from the cart
tail, sniffed the smoke of Edinboro' town and
faced right about. To the farmer's peremptory
call he returned the spicy repartee of a cheerful
bark. It was as much as to say:

"Dinna fash yersel'! I ken what I'm aboot."

After an hour's hard run back over the dipping
and rising country road and a long quarter-
circuit of the city, Bobby found the high-walled,
winding way into the west end of the Grassmarket
To a human being afoot there was a shorter cut,
but the little dog could only retrace the familiar
route of the farm carts. It was a notable feat
for a small creature whose tufted legs were not
more than six inches in length, whose thatch ol
long hair almost swept the roadway and caught
at every burr and bramble, and who was still so
young that his nose could not be said to be
educated.

In the market-place he ran here and there through the crowd, hopefully investigating narrow closes that were mere rifts in precipices of buildings; nosing outside stairs, doorways, stables, bridge arches, standing carts, and even hob-nailed boots. He yelped at the crash of the gun, but it was another matter altogether that set his little heart to palpitating with alarm. It was the dinner-hour, and where was Auld Jock?

Ah! A happy thought: his master had gone to dinner!

A human friend would have resented the idea of such base desertion and sulked. But in a little dog's heart of trust there is no room for suspicion. The thought simply lent wings to Bobby's tired feet. As the market-place emptied he chased at the heels of laggards, up the crescent-shaped rise of Candlemakers Row, and straight on to the familiar dining-rooms. Through the forest of table and chair and human legs he made his way to the back, to find a soldier from the Castle, in smart red coat and polished boots, lounging in Auld Jock's inglenook.

Bobby stood stock still for a shocked instant. Then he howled dismally and bolted for the door. Mr. John Traill, the smooth-shaven, hatchet-faced proprietor, standing midway in shirt-sleeves and white apron, caught the flying terrier between his legs and gave him a friendly clap on the side.

"Did you come by your ainsel' with a farthing in your silky-purse ear to buy a bone, Bobby? Whaur's Auld Jock?"

A fear may be crowded back into the mind and stoutly denied so long as it is not named. At the good landlord's very natural question: "Whaur's Auld Jock?" there was the shape of the little dog's fear that he had lost his master. With a whimpering cry he struggled free. Out of the door he went, like a shot. He tumbled down the steep curve and doubled on his tracks around the market-place.

At his onslaught, the sparrows rose like brown leaves on a gust of wind, and drifted down again. A cold mist veiled the Castle heights. From the stone crown of the ancient Cathedral of St. Giles, on High Street, floated the melody of "The Bluebells of Scotland." No day was too bleak for bell-ringer McLeod to climb the shaking ladder in the windy tower and play the music bells during the hour that Edinburgh dined. Bobby forgot to dine that day, first in his distracted search, and then in his joy of finding his master.

For, all at once, in the very strangest place, in the very strangest way, Bobby came upon Auld Jock. A rat. scurrying out from a foul and narrow passage that gave to the rear of the White Hart Inn, pointed the little dog to a nook hitherto undiscovered by his curious nose. Hidden away between the noisy tavern and the grim, island crag was the old cock-fighting pit of a ruder day. There, in a broken-down carrier's cart, abandoned among the nameless abominations of public-house refuse, Auld Jock lay huddled in his great-coat of hodden gray and his shepherd's plaid. On a bundle of clothing tied in a tartan ker-chief for a pillow, he lay very still and breathing heavily.

Bobby barked as if he would burst his lungs. He barked so long, so loud, and so furiously, running 'round and 'round the cart and under it and yelping at every turn, that a slatternly scullery maid opened a door and angrily bade him "no' to deave folk wi' 'is blatterin'." Auld Jock she did not see at all in the murky pit or, if she saw him, thought him some drunken foreign sailor from Leith harbor. When she went in, she slammed the door and lighted the gas.

Whether from some instinct of protection of his helpless master in that foul and hostile place, or because barking had proved to be of no use, Bobby sat back on his haunches and considered this strange, disquieting thing. It was not like Auld Jock to sleep in the daytime, or so soundly,

GREYFRIARS BOBBY

at any time, that barking would not awaken him.
A clever and resourceful dog, Bobby crouched
back against the farthest wall, took a running
leap to the top of the low boots, dug his claws
into the stout, home-knitted stockings, and
scrambled up over Auld Jock's legs into the cart.
In an instant he poked his little black mop of a
wet muzzle into his master's face and barked
once, sharply, in his ear.

To Bobby's delight Auld Jock sat up and
blinked his eyes. The old eyes were brighter,
the grizzled face redder than was natural, but
such matters were quite outside of the little dog's
ken. It was a dazed moment before the man remembered that Bobby should not be there. He
frowned down at the excited little creature, who
was wagging satisfaction from his nose-tip to the
end of his crested tail, in a puzzled effort to
remember why.

"Eh, Bobby!" His tone was one of vague
reproof. "Nae doot ye're fair satisfied wi' yer
ainsel'."

Bobby's feathered tail drooped, but it still
quivered, all ready to wag again at the slightest
encouragement. Auld Jock stared at him stu-
pidly, his dizzy head in his hands. A very tired,
very draggled little dog, Bobby dropped beside
his master, panting, subdued by the reproach,

15

but happy. His soft eyes, veiled by the silvery fringe that fell from his high forehead, were deep-brown pools of affection. Auld Jock forgot, by and by, that Bobby should not be there, and felt only the comfort of his companionship.

"Weel, Bobby," he began again, uncertainly. And then, because his Scotch peasant reticence had been quite broken down by Bobby's shameless devotion, so that he told the little dog many things that he cannily concealed from human kind, he confided the strange weakness and dizziness in the head that had overtaken him: "Auld Jock is juist fair silly the day, bonny wee laddie."

Down came a shaking, hot old hand in a rough caress, and up a gallant young tail to wave like a banner. All was right with the little dog's world again. But it was plain, even to Bobby, that something had gone wrong with Auld Jock. It was the man who wore the air of a culprit. A Scotch laborer does not lightly confess to feeling "fair silly," nor sleep away the busy hours of daylight. The old man was puzzled and humiliated by this discreditable thing. A human friend would have understood his plight, led the fevered man out of that bleak and fetid cul-de-sac, tucked him into a warm bed, comforted him with a hot drink, and then gone swiftly for

skilled help.   Bobby knew only that his master
had unusual need of love.

Very, very early a dog learns that life is not as
simple a matter to his master as it is to himself.
There are times when he reads trouble, that he
cannot help or understand, in the man's eye and
voice.   Then he can only look his love and
loyalty, wistfully, as if he felt his own short-
coming in the matter of speech.   And if the
trouble is so great that the master forgets to eat
his dinner; forgets, also, the needs of his faithful
little friend, it is the dog's dear privilege to bear
neglect and hunger without complaint.   Therefore, when Auld Jock lay down again and sank,
almost at once, into sodden sleep, Bobby snuggled in the hollow of his master's arm and
nuzzled his nose in his master's neck.

II

WHILE the bells played "There Grows a Bonny Briarbush in Our Kale Yard" Auld Jock and Bobby slept. They slept while the tavern emptied itself of noisy guests and clattering crockery was washed at the dingy, gas-lighted windows that overlooked the cockpit. They slept while the cold fell with the falling day and the mist was whipped into driving rain. Almost a cave, between shelving rock and house wall, a gust of wind still found its way in now and then. At a splash of rain Auld Jock stirred uneasily in his sleep. Bobby merely sniffed the freshened air with pleasure and curled himself up for another nap.

No rain could wet Bobby. Under his rough outer coat, that was parted along the back as neatly as the thatch along a cottage ridge-pole, was a dense, woolly fleece that defied wind and rain, snow and sleet to penetrate. He could not know that nature had not been as generous in protecting his master against the weather. Although of a subarctic breed, fitted to live shelter

less if need be, and to earn his living by native
wit, Bobby had the beauty, the grace, and the
charming manners of a lady's pet. In a litter
of prick-eared, wire-haired puppies Bobby was
a "sport."

It is said that some of the ships of the Spanish
Armada, with French poodles in the officers'
cabins, were blown far north and west, and
broken up on the icy coasts of The Hebrides and
Skye. Some such crossing of his far-away an-
cestry, it would seem, had given a greater length
and a crisp wave to Bobby's outer coat, dropped
and silkily fringed his ears, and powdered his useful, slate-gray color with silver frost. But he
had the hardiness and intelligence of the sturdier
breed, and the instinct of devotion to the working
master. So he had turned from a soft-hearted
bit lassie of a mistress, and the cozy chimney-
corner of the farm-house kitchen, and linked his
fortunes with this forlorn old laborer.

A grizzled, gnarled little man was Auld Jock, of
tough fiber, but worn out at last by fifty winters
as a shepherd on the bleak hills of Midlothian
and Fife, and a dozen more in the low stables and
storm-buffeted garrets of Edinburgh. He had
come into the world unnoted in a shepherd's
lonely cot. With little wit of mind or skill of
hand he had been a common tool, used by this

master and that for the roughest tasks, when needed, put aside, passed on, and dropped out of mind. Nothing ever belonged to the man but his scant earnings. Wifeless, cotless, bairnless, he had slept, since early boyhood, under strange roofs, eaten the bread of the hireling, and sat dumb at other men's firesides. If he had another name it had been forgotten. In youth he was Jock; in age, Auld Jock.

In his sixty-third summer there was a belated blooming in Auld Jock's soul. Out of some miraculous caprice Bobby lavished on him a riotous affection. Then up out of the man's subconscious memory came words learned from the lips of a long-forgotten mother. They were words not meant for little dogs at all, ·at for sweetheart, wife and bairn. Auld Jock used them cautiously, fearing to be overheard, for the matter was a subject of wonder and rough jest at the farm. He used them when Bobby followed him at the plow-tail or scampered over the heather with him behind the flocks. He used them on the market-day journeyings, and on summer nights, when the sea wind came sweetly from the broad Firth and the two slept, like ·agabonds, on a haycock under the stars. The purest pleasure Auld Jock ever knew was the taking of a bright farthing from his pocket to pay for Bobby's delectable bone in Mr. Traill's place.

Given what was due him that morning and dismissed for the season to find such work as he could in the city, Auld Jock did not question the farmer's right to take Bobby "back hame." Besides, what could he do with the noisy little rascal in an Edinburgh lodging? But, duller of wit than usual, feeling very old and lonely, and shaky on his legs, and dizzy in his head, Auld Jock parted with Bobby and with his courage, together. With the instinct of the dumb animal that suffers, he stumbled into the foul nook and fell, almost at once, into a heavy sleep. Out of that Bobby roused him but briefly.

Long before his master awoke, Bobby finished his series of refreshing little naps, sat up, yawned, stretched his short, shaggy legs, sniffed at Auld Jock experimentally, and trotted around the bed of the cart on a tour of investigation. This proving to be of small interest and no profit, he lay down again beside his master, nose on paws, and waited Auld Jock's pleasure patiently. A sweep of drenching rain brought the old man suddenly to his feet and stumbling into the market-place. The alert little dog tumbled about him, barking ecstatically. The fever was gone and Auld Jock's head quite clear; but in its place was a weakness, an aching of the limbs, a weight on the chest, and a great shivering.

Although the bell of St. Giles was just striking the hour of five, it was already entirely dark. A lamp-lighter, with ladder and torch, was setting a double line of gas-jets to flaring along the lofty parapets of the bridge. If the Grassmarket was a quarry pit by day, on a night of storm it was the bottom of a reservoir. The height of the walls was marked by a luminous crown from many lights above the Castle head, and by a student's dim candle, here and there, at a garret window. The huge bulk of the bridge cast a shadow, velvet black, across the eastern half of the market.

Had not Bobby gone before and barked, and run back, again and again, and jumped up on Auld Jock's legs, the man might never have won his way across the drowned place, in the inky black-ness and against the slanted blast of icy rain. When he gained the foot of Candlemakers Row, a crescent of tall, old houses that curved upward around the lower end of Greyfriars kirkyard, water poured upon him from the heavy timbered gallery of the Cunzie Neuk, once the royal mint. The carting office that occupied the street floor was closed, or Auld Jock would have sought shelter there. He struggled up the rise, made slippery by rain and grime. Then, as the street turned southward in its easy curve, there was some shelter from the house walls. But Auld Jock was quite exhausted and incapable of caring for himself. In the ancient guildhall of the candlemakers, at the top of the Row, was another carting office and Harrow Inn, a resort of country carriers. The man would have gone in there where he was quite unknown or, indeed, he might even have lain down in the bleak court that gave access to the tenements above, but for Bobby's persistent and cheerful barking, begging and nipping.

"Maister, maister!" he said, as plainly as a little dog could speak, "dinna bide here. It's juist a stap or twa to food an' fire i' the cozy auld ingleneuk."

And then, the level roadway won at last, there was the railing of the bridge-approach to cling to, on the one hand, and the upright bars of the kirkyard gate on the other. By the help of these and the urging of wee Bobby, Auld Jock came the short, steep way up out of the market, to the row of lighted shops in Greyfriars Place.

With the wind at the back and above the housetops, Mr. Traill stood bare-headed in a dry haven of peace in his doorway, firelight behind him, and welcome in his shrewd gray eyes. If Auld Jock had shown any intention of going by.

it is not impossible that the landlord of Ye Olde Greyfriars Dining-Rooms might have dragged him in bodily. The storm had driven all his customers home. For an hour there had not been a soul in the place to speak to, and it was so entirely necessary for John Traill to hear his own voice that he had been known, in such straits, to talk to himself. Auld Jock was not an inspiring auditor, but a deal better than naething; and, if he proved hopeless, entertainment was to be found in Bobby. So Mr. Traill bustled in before his guests, poked the open fire into leaping flames, and heaped it up skilfully at the back with fresh coals. The good landlord turned from his hospitable task to find Auld Jock streaming and shaking on the hearth.

"Man, but you're wet!" he exclaimed. He hustled the old shepherd out of his dripping plaid and greatcoat and spread them to the blaze. Auld Jock found a dry, knitted Tam-o'-Shanter bonnet in his little bundle and set it on his head. It was a moment or two before he could speak without the humiliating betrayal of chattering teeth.

"Ay, it's a misty nicht," he admitted, with caution.

"Misty! Man, it's raining like all the seven deils were abroad." Having delivered himself of

24

this violent opinion, Mr. Traill fell into his usual philosophic vein. "I have sma' patience with the Scotch way of making little of everything. If Noah had been a Lowland Scot he'd 'a' said the deluge was 'juist fair wat.'"

He laughed at his own wit, his thin-featured face and keen gray eyes lighting up to a kindliness that his brusque speech denied in vain. He had a fluency of good English at command that he would have thought ostentatious to use in speaking with a simple country body.

Auld Jock stared at Mr. Traill and pondered the matter. By and by he asked: "Wasna the deluge fair wat?"

The landlord sighed but, brought to book like that, admitted that it was. Conversation flagged, however, while he busied himself with toasting a smoked herring, and dragging roasted potatoes from the little iron oven that was fitted into the brickwork of the fireplace beside the grate.

Bobby was attending to his own entertainment. The familiar place wore a new and enchanting aspect, and needed instant exploration. By day it was fitted with tables, picketed by chairs and all manner of boots. Noisy and crowded, a little dog that wandered about there was liable to be trodden upon. On that night of storm it was a vast, bright place, so silent one could hear the

ticking of the wag-at-the-wa' clock, the crisp
crackling of the flames, and the snapping of the
coals. The uncovered deal tables were set back
in a double line along one wall, with the chairs
piled on top, leaving a wide passage of freshly
scrubbed and sanded oaken floor from the door
to the fireplace. Firelight danced on the dark
old wainscoting and high, carved overmantel,
winked on rows of drinking-mugs and metal
covers over cold meats on the buffet, and even
picked out the gilt titles on the backs of a shelf
of books in Mr. Traill's private corner behind the
bar.

Bobby shook himself on the hearth to free his
rain-coat of surplus water. To the landlord's
dry "We're no' needing a shower in the house.
Lie down, Bobby," he wagged his tail politely, as
a sign that he heard. But, as Auld Jock did not
repeat the order, he ignored it and scampered
busily about the room, leaving little trails of wet
behind him.

This grill-room of Traill's place was more like
the parlor of a country inn, or a farm-house
kitchen if there had been a built-in bed or two,
than a restaurant in the city. There, a humble
man might see his herring toasted, his bannocks
baked on the oven-top, or his tea brewed to his
liking. On such a night as this the landlord

would pull the settle out of the inglenook to the hearth, set before the solitary guest a small table, and keep the kettle on the hob.

"Spread yoursel' on both sides o' the fire, man. There'll be nane to keep us company, I'm thinking. Ilka man that has a roof o' his ain will be wearing it for a bonnet the nicht."

As there was no answer to this, the skilled conversational angler dropped a bit of bait that the wariest man must rise to.

"That's a vera intelligent bit dog, Auld Jock. He was here with the time-gun spiering for you. When he didna find you he greeted like a bairn."

Auld Jock, huddled in the corner of the settle, so near the fire that his jacket smoked, took so long a time to find an answer that Mr. Traill looked at him keenly as he set the wooden plate and pewter mug on the table.

"Man, you're vera ill," he cried, sharply. In truth he was shocked and self-accusing because he had not observed Auld Jock's condition before.

"I'm no' so awfu' ill," came back in irritated denial, as if he had been accused of some misbehavior.

"Weel, it's no' a dry herrin' ye'll hae in my shop the nicht. It's a hot mutton broo wi' porridge in it, an' bits o' meat to tak' the cauld oot o' yer auld banes."

And there, the plate was whisked away, and the cover lifted from a bubbling pot, and the kettle was over the fire for the brewing of tea. At a peremptory order the soaked boots and stockings were off, and dry socks found in the kerchief bundle. Auld Jock was used to taking orders from his superiors, and offered no resistance to being hustled after this manner into warmth and good cheer. Besides, who could have withstood that flood of homely speech on which the good landlord came right down to the old shepherd's humble level? Such warm feeling was established that Mr. Traill quite forgot his usual caution and certain well-known prejudices of old country bodies.

"Noo," he said cheerfully, as he set the hot broth on the table, "ye maun juist hae a doctor."

A doctor is the last resort of the unlettered poor. The very threat of one to the Scotch peasant of a half-century ago was a sentence of death. Auld Jock blanched, and he shook so that he dropped his spoon. Mr. Traill hastened to undo the mischief.

"It's no' a doctor ye'll be needing, ava, but a bit dose o' physic an' a bed in the infirmary a day or twa."

"I wullna gang to the infairmary. It's juist for puir toon bodies that are aye ailin' an' deein'.'

Fright and resentment lent the silent old man
an astonishing eloquence for the moment. "Ye
wadna gang to the infairmary yer ainsel', an'
tak' charity."

"Would I no'? I would go if I so much as
cut my sma' finger; and I would let a student
laddie bind it up for me."

"Weel, ye're a saft ane," said Auld Jock.

It was a terrible word—"saft!" John Traill
flushed darkly, and relapsed into discouraged
silence. Deep down in his heart he knew that
a regiment of soldiers from the Castle could not
take him alive, a free patient, into the infirmary.
But what was one to do but "lee," right heartily,
for the good of this very sick, very poor, homeless old man on a night of pitiless storm? That
he had "lee'd" to no purpose and got a "saft"
name for it was a blow to his pride.

Hearing the clatter of fork and spoon, Bobby
trotted from behind the bar and saved the day
of discomfiture. Time for dinner, indeed! Up
he came on his hind legs and politely begged his
master for food. It was the prettiest thing he
could do, and the landlord delighted in him.

"Gie 'im a penny plate o' the gude broo," said
Auld Jock, and he took the copper coin from
his pocket to pay for it. He forgot his own
belated meal in watching the hungry little

creature eat. Warmed and softened by Mr.
Traill's kindness, and by the heartening food,
Auld Jock betrayed a thought that had rankled
in the depths of his mind all day.

"Bobby isna ma ain dog." His voice was dull
and unhappy.

Ah, here was misery deeper than any physical
ill! The penny was his, a senseless thing; but,
poor, old, sick, hameless and kinless, the little
dog that loved and followed him "wasna his
ain." To hide the huskiness in his own voice
Mr. Traill relapsed into broad, burr-y Scotch.

"Dinna fash yersel', man. The wee beastie is
maist mighty fond o' ye, an' ilka dog aye chooses
'is ain maister."

Auld Jock shook his head and gave a brie
account of Bobby's perversity. On the ver
next market-day the little dog must be restored
to the tenant of Cauldbrae farm and, if necessary,
tied in the cart. It was unlikely, young as he
was, that he would try to find his way back, all
the way from near the top of the Pentlands.
In a day or two he would forget Auld Jock.

"I canna say it wullna be sair partin'—" And
then, seeing the sympathy in the landlord's eye
and fearing a disgraceful breakdown, Auld Jock
checked his self-betrayal. During the talk
Bobby stood listening. At the abrupt ending

he put his shagged paws up on Auld Jock's knee, wistfully inquiring about this emotional matter. Then he dropped soberly, and slunk away under his master's chair.

"Ay, he kens we're talkin' aboot 'im."

"He's a knowing bit dog. Have you attended to his sairous education, man?"

"Nae, he's ower young."

"Young is aye the time to teach a dog or a bairn that life is no' all play. Man, you should put a sma' terrier at the vermin an' mak' him usefu'."

"It's eneugh, gin he's gude company for the wee lassie wha's fair fond o' 'im," Auld Jock answered, briefly. This was a strange sentiment from the work-broken old man who, for himself, would have held ornamental idleness sinful. He finished his supper in brooding silence. At last he broke out in a peevish irritation that only made his grief at parting with Bobby more apparent to an understanding man like Mr. Traill.

"I dinna ken what to do wi' 'im i' an Edinburgh lodgin' the nicht. The auld wifie I lodge wi' is dour by the ordinar', an' wadna bide 'is blatterin'. I couldna get 'im past 'er auld een, an' thae terriers are aye barkin' aboot naethin' ava."

Mr. Traill's eyes sparkled at recollection of an

apt literary story to which Dr. John Brown had given currency. Like many Edinburgh shop-keepers, Mr. Traill was a man of superior educa-tion and an omnivorous reader. And he had many customers from the near-by University to give him a fund of stories of Scotch writers and other worthies.

"You have a double plaid, man?"

"Ay. Ilka shepherd's got a twa-fold plaidie." It seemed a foolish question to Auld Jock, but Mr. Traill went on blithely.

"There's a pocket in the plaid—ane end left open at the side to mak' a pouch? Nae doubt you've carried mony a thing in that pouch?"

"Nae; no' so mony. Juist the new-born lambs."

"Weel, Sir Walter had a shepherd's plaid, and there was a bit lassie he was vera fond of. Syne, when he had been at the writing a' the day, and was aff his heid like, with too mony thoughts, he'd go across the town and fetch the bairnie to keep him company. She was a weel-born lassie, sax or seven years auld, and sma' of her age, but no' half as sma' as Bobby, I'm thinking." He stopped to let this significant comparison sink into Auld Jock's mind. "The lassie had nae liking for the unmannerly wind and snaw of Edinburgh. So Sir Walter just

happed her in the pouch of his plaid, and tumbled her out, snug as a lamb and nane the wiser,
in the big room wha's walls were lined with
books."

Auld Jock betrayed not a glimmer of intelligence as to the personal bearing of the story,
but he showed polite interest. "I ken naethin'
aboot Sir Walter or ony o' the grand folk." Mr.
Traill sighed, cleared the table in silence, and
mended the fire. It was ill having no one to
talk to but a simple old body who couldn't put
two and two together and make four.

The landlord lighted his pipe meditatively, and
he lighted his cruisey lamp for reading. Auld
Jock was dry and warm again; oh, very, very
warm, so that he presently fell into a doze. The
dining-room was so compassed on all sides but the
front by neighboring house and kirkyard wall
and by the floors above, that only a murmur of
the storm penetrated it. It was so quiet, indeed,
that a tiny, scratching sound in a distant corner
was heard distinctly. A streak of dark silver,
as of animated mercury, Bobby flashed past.
A scuffle, a squeak, and he was back again,
dropping a big rat at the landlord's feet and
wagging his tail with pride.

"Weel done, Bobby! There's a bite and a
bone for you here ony time o' day you call for it.

Ay, a sensible bit dog will attend to his ain education and mak' himsel' usefu'.''

Mr. Traill felt a sudden access of warm liking
for the attractive little scrap of knowingness and
pluck. He patted the tousled head, but Bobby
backed away. He had no mind to be caressed by
any man beside his master. After a moment
the landlord took *Guy Mannering* down from the
book-shelf. Knowing his *Waverley* by heart, he
turned at once to the passages about Dandie
Dinmont and his terriers—Mustard and Pepper
and other spicy wee rascals.

"Ay, terriers are sonsie, leal dogs. Auld Jock
will have ane true mourner at his funeral. I
would no' mind if—"

On impulse he got up and dropped a couple
of hard Scotch buns, very good dog-biscuit,
indeed, into the pocket of Auld Jock's greatcoat
for Bobby. The old man might not be able to
be out the morn. With the thought in his mind
that some one should keep a friendly eye on the
man, he mended the fire with such an unnecessary
clattering of the tongs that Auld Jock started
from his sleep with a cry.

"Whaur is it you have your lodging, Jock?"
the landlord asked, sharply, for the man looked
so dazed that his understanding was not to be
reached easily. He got the indefinite informa-

tion that it was at the top of one of the tall, old tenements "juist aff the Coogate."

"A lang climb for an auld man," John Traill said, compassionately; then, optimistic as usual, "but it's a lang climb or a foul smell, in the poor quarters of Edinburgh."

"Ay. It's weel aboon the fou' smell." With some comforting thought that he did not confide to Mr. Traill, but that ironed lines out of his old face, Auld Jock went to sleep again. Well, the landlord reflected, he could remain there by the fire until the closing hour or later, if need be, and by that time the storm might ease a bit, so that he could get to his lodging without another wetting.

For an hour the place was silent, except for the falling clinkers from the grate, the rustling of book-leaves, and the plumping of rain on the windows, when the wind shifted a point. Lost in the romance, Mr. Traill took no note of the passing time or of his quiet guests until he felt a little tug at his trouser-leg.

"Eh, laddie?" he questioned. Up the little dog rose in the begging attitude. Then, with a sharp bark, he dashed back to his master.

Something was very wrong, indeed. Auld Jock had sunk down in his seat. His arms hung helplessly over the end and back of the settle, and his legs were sprawled limply before him The bonnet that he always wore, outdoors and in, had fallen from his scant, gray locks, and his head had dropped forward on his chest. His breathing was labored, and he muttered in his sleep.

In a moment Mr. Traill was inside his own greatcoat, storm boots and bonnet. At the door he turned back. The shop was unguarded. Although Greyfriars Place lay on the hilltop, with the sanctuary of the kirkyard behind it, and the University at no great distance in front, it was but a step up from the thief-infested gorge of the Cowgate. The landlord locked his money-drawer, pushed his easy-chair against it, and roused Auld Jock so far as to move him over from the settle. The chief responsibility he laid on the anxious little dog, that watched his every movement.

"Lie down, Bobby, and mind Auld Jock. And you're no' a gude dog if you canna bark to waken the dead in the kirkyard, if ony strange body comes about."

"Whaur are ye gangin'?" cried Auld Jock. He was wide awake, with burning, suspicious eyes fixed on his host.

"Sit you down, man, with your back to my siller. I'm going for a doctor." The noise of the storm, as he opened the door, prevented his hearing the frightened protest:

"Dinna gang!"

The rain had turned to sleet, and Mr. Traill had trouble in keeping his feet. He looked first into the famous Book Hunter's Stall next door, on the chance of finding a medical student. The place was open, but it had no customers. He went on to the bridge, but there the sheriff's court, the Martyr's church, the society halls and all the smart shops were closed, their dark fronts lighted fitfully by flaring gas-lamps. The bitter night had driven all Edinburgh to private cover.

From the rear came a clear whistle. Some Heriot laddie who, being not entirely a "puir orphan," but only "faderless" and, therefore, living outside the school with his mother, had been kept after nightfall because of ill-prepared lessons or misbehavior. Mr. Traill turned, passed his own door, and went on southward into Forest Road, that skirted the long arm of the kirkyard.

From the Burghmuir, all the way to the Grassmarket and the Cowgate, was downhill. So, with arms winged, and stout legs spread wide and braced, Geordie Ross was sliding gaily homeward, his knitted tippet a gallant pennant behind. Here was a Mercury for an urgent errand.

"Laddie, do you know whaur's a doctor who

can be had for a shulling or two for a poor auld
country body in my shop?"

"Is he so awfu' ill?" Geordie asked with the
morbid curiosity of lusty boyhood.

"He's a' that. He's aff his heid. Run,
laddie, and dinna be standing there wagging your
fule tongue for naething."

Geordie was off with speed across the bridge
to High Street. Mr. Traill struggled back to his
shop, against wind and treacherous ice, thinking
what kind of a bed might be contrived for the
sick man for the night. In the morning the daft
auld body could be hurried, willy-nilly, to a bed
in the infirmary. As for wee Bobby he wouldn't
mind if—

And there he ran into his own wide-flung door.
A gale blew through the hastily deserted place.
Ashes were scattered about the hearth, and the
cruisey lamp flared in the gusts. Auld Jock and
Bobby were gone.

III

ALTHOUGH dismayed and self-accusing for having frightened Auld Jock into taking flight by his incautious talk of a doctor, not for an instant did the landlord of Greyfriars Dining-Rooms entertain the idea of following him. The old man had only to cross the street and drop down the incline between the bridge-approach and the ancient Chapel of St. Magdalen to be lost in the deepest, most densely peopled, and blackest gorge in Christendom.

Well knowing that he was safe from pursuit, Auld Jock chuckled as he gained the last low level. Fever lent him a brief strength, and the cold damp was grateful to his hot skin. None were abroad in the Cowgate; and that was lucky for, in this black hole of Edinburgh, even so old and poor a man was liable to be set upon by thieves, on the chance of a few shillings or pence.

Used as he was to following flocks up treacherous braes and through drifted glens, and sure-footed as a collie, Auld Jock had to pick his way carefully over the slimy, ice-glazed cobblestones of the Cowgate. He could see nothing The scattered gas-lamps, blurred by the wet, only made a timbered gallery or stone stairs stand out here and there or lighted up a Gothic gargoyle to a fantastic grin. The street lay so deep and narrow that sleet and wind wasted little time in finding it out, but roared and rattled among the gables, dormers and chimney-stacks overhead. Happy in finding his master himself again, and sniffing fresh adventure, Bobby tumbled noisily about Auld Jock's feet until reproved. And here was strange going. Ancient and warring smells confused and insulted the little country dog's nose. After a few inquiring and protesting barks Bobby fell into a subdued trot at Auld Jock's heels.

To this shepherd in exile the romance of Old Edinburgh was a sealed book. It was, indeed, difficult for the most imaginative to believe that the Cowgate was once a lovely, wooded ravine, with a rustic burn babbling over pebbles at its bottom, and along the brook a straggling path worn smooth by cattle on their driven way to the Grassmarket. Then, when the Scotish nobility was crowded out of the piled-up mansions, on the sloping ridge of High Street that ran the mile from the Castle to Holyrood Palace, splendor camped in the Cowgate, in villas set in fair gardens, and separated by hedge-rows in which birds nested.

In time this ravine, too, became overbuilt. Houses tumbled down both slopes to the winding cattle path, and the burn was arched over to make a thoroughfare. Laterally, the buildings were crowded together, until the upper floors were pushed out on timber brackets for light and air. Galleries, stairs and jutting windows were added to outer walls, and the mansions climbed, storey above storey, until the Cowgate was an undercut cañon, such as is worn through rock by the rivers of western America. Lairds and leddies, powdered, jeweled and satin-shod, were borne in sedan chairs down ten flights of stone stairs and through torch-lit courts and tunnel streets, to routs in Castle or Palace and to tourneys in the Grassmarket.

From its low situation the Cowgate came in the course of time to smell to heaven, and out of it was a sudden exodus of grand folk to the northern hills. The lowest level was given over at once to the poor and to small trade. The wynds and closes that climbed the southern slope were eagerly possessed by divines, lawyers and literary men because of their nearness to the University. Long before Bobby's day the well-to-do had fled from the Cowgate wynds to the hilltop streets and open squares about the colleges. A few decent working-men remained in the decaying houses, some of which were at least three centuries old. But there swarmed in upon, and submerged them, thousands of criminals, beggars, and the miserably poor and degraded of many nationalities. Businesses that fatten on misfortune—the saloon, pawn, old clothes and cheap food shops—lined the squalid Cowgate. Palaces were cut up into honeycombs of tall tenements. Every stair was a crowded highway; every passage a place of deposit for filth; almost every room sheltered a half-famished family, in darkness and ancient dirt. Grand and great, pious and wise, decent, wretched and terrible folk, of every sort, had preceded Auld Jock to his lodging in a steep and narrow wynd, and nine gusty flights up under a beautiful, old Gothic gable.

A wrought-iron lantern hanging in an arched opening, lighted the entrance to the wynd. With a hand outstretched to either wall Auld Jock felt his way up. Another lantern marked a sculptured doorway that gave to the foul court of the tenement. No sky could be seen above the open well of the court, and the carved, oaken bannister of the stairs had to be felt for and clung to by one so short of breath. On the seventh

landing, from the exertion of the long climb,
Auld Jock was shaken into helplessness, and his
heart set to pounding, by a violent fit of coughing. Overhead a shutter was slammed back, and
an angry voice bade him stop "deaving folk."

The last two flights ascended within the walls.
The old man stumbled into the pitch-black,
stifling passage and sat down on the lowest step
to rest. On the landing above he must encounter
the auld wifie of a landlady, rousing her, it might
be, and none too good-tempered, from sleep.
Unaware that he added to his master's difficulties, Bobby leaped upon him and licked the beloved face that he could not see.

"Eh, laddie, I dinna ken what to do wi' ye.
We maun juist hae to sleep oot." It did not
occur to Auld Jock that he could abandon the
little dog. And then there drifted across his
memory a bit of Mr. Traill's talk that, at the
time, had seemed to no purpose: "Sir Walter
happed the wee lassie in the pocket of his
plaid—" He slapped his knee in silent triumph.
In the dark he found the broad, open end of the
plaid, and the rough, excited head of the little
dog.

"A hap, an' a stap, an' a loup, an' in ye gang.
Loup in, laddie!"

Bobby jumped into the pocket and turned

'round and 'round. His little muzzle opened for a delighted bark at this original play, but Auld Jock checked him.

"Cuddle doon noo, an' lie canny as pussy." With a deft turn he brought the weighted end of the plaid up under his arm so there would be no betraying drag. "We'll pu' the wool ower the auld wifie's een," he chuckled.

He mounted the stairs almost blithely, and knocked on one of the three narrow doors that opened on the two-by-eight landing. It was opened a few inches, on a chain, and a sordid old face, framed in straggling gray locks and a dirty mutch cap, peered suspiciously at him through the crevice.

Auld Jock had his money in hand—a shilling and a sixpence—to pay for a week's lodging. He had slept in this place for several winters, and the old woman knew him well, but she held his coins to the candle and bit them with her teeth to test them. Without a word of greeting she shoved the key to the sleeping-closet he had always fancied, through the crack in the door, and pointed to a jug of water at the foot of the attic stairs. On the proffer of a halfpenny she gave him a tallow candle, lighted it at her own and fitted it into the neck of a beer bottle.

"Ye hae a cauld," she said at last, with some

hostility. "Gin ye wauken yer neebors ye'll juist hae to techt it oot wi' 'em."

"Ay, I ken a' that," Auld Jock answered. He smothered a cough in his chest with such effort that it threw him into a perspiration. In some way, with the jug of water and the lighted candle in his hands and the hidden terrier under one arm, the old man mounted the eighteen-inch-wide, walled-in attic stairs and unlocked the first of a number of narrow doors on the passage at the top.

"Weel aboon the fou' smell," indeed; "weel worth the lang climb!" Around the loose frames of two wee southward-looking dormer windows, that jutted from the slope of the gable, came a gush of rain-washed air. Auld Jock tumbled Bobby, warm and happy and "nane the wiser," out into the cold cell of a room that was oh, so very, very different from the high, warm, richly colored library of Sir Walter! This garret closet in the slums of Edinburgh was all of cut stone, except for the worn, oaken floor, a flimsy, modern door, and a thin, board partition on one side through which a "neebor" could be heard snoring. Filling all of the outer wall, between the peephole, leaded windows and running up to the slope of the ceiling, was a great fireplace of native white freestone, carved into fluted col-

umns, foliated capitals, and a fiat pediment of
purest classic lines. The ballroom of a noble
of Queen Mary's day had been cut up into numerous small sleeping-closets, many of them
windowless, and were let to the chance lodger at
threepence the night. Here, where generations
of dancing toes had been warmed, the chimney-
vent was bricked up, and a boxed-in shelf fitted,
to serve for a bed, a seat and a table, for such
as had neither time nor heart for dancing. For
the romantic history and the beauty of it, Auld
Jock had no mind at all. But, ah! he had other
joy often missed by the more fortunate.

"Be canny, Bobby," he cautioned again.

The sagacious little dog understood, and pat-
tered about the place silently. Exhausting it in
a moment, and very plainly puzzled and bored,
he sat on his haunches, yawned wide, and looked
up inquiringly to his master. Auld Jock set the
jug and the candle on the floor and slipped off
his boots. He had no wish to "wauken 'is
neebors." With nervous haste he threw back one
of the windows on its hinges, reached across the
wide stone ledge and brought in—wonder of
wonders, in such a place—a tiny earthen pot of
heather!

"Is it no' a bonny posie?" he whispered to
Bobby. With this cherished bit of the country

that he had left behind him the April before in his hands, he sat down in the fireplace bed and lifted Bobby beside him.   He sniffed at the withered tuft of purple bloom fondly, and his old face blossomed into smiles.   It was the secret thought of this, and of the hillward outlook from the little windows, that had ironed the lines from his face in Mr. Traill's dining-room.   Bobby sniffed at the starved plant, too, and wagged his tail with pleasure, for a dog's keenest memories are recorded by the nose.

Overhead, loose tiles and finials rattled in the wind, that was dying away in fitful gusts; but Auld Jock heard nothing.   In fancy he was away on the braes, in the shy sun and wild wet of April weather.   Shepherds were shouting, sheep-dogs barking, ewes bleating, and a wee puppy, still unnamed, scampering at his heels in the swift, dramatic days of lambing time.   And so, presently, when the forlorn hope of the little pot had been restored to the ledge, master and dog were in tune with the open country, and began a romp such as they often had indulged in behind the byre on a quiet, Sabbath afternoon.

They had learned to play there like two well-brought-up children, in pantomime, so as not to scandalize pious countryfolk.   Now, in obedience to a gesture, a nod, a lifted eyebrow,

Bobby went through all his pretty tricks, and showed how far his serious education had pro-gressed. He rolled over and over, begged, vaulted the low hurdle of his master's arm, and played "deid." He scampered madly over imaginary pastures; ran, straight as a string, along a stone wall; scrambled under a thorny hedge; chased rabbits, and dug foxes out of holes; swam a burn, flushed feeding curlews, and "froze" beside a rat-hole. When the excitement was at its height and the little dog was bursting with exuberance, Auld Jock forgot his caution. Holding his bonnet just out of reach, he cried aloud:

"Loup, Bobby!"

Bobby jumped for the bonnet, missed it, jumped again and barked—the high-pitched, penetrating yelp of the terrier.

Instantly their little house of joy tumbled about their ears. There was a pounding on the thin partition wall, an oath and a shout: "Whaur's the deil o' a dog?" Bobby flew at the insulting clamor, but Auld Jock dragged him back roughly. In a voice made harsh by fear for his little pet, he commanded

"Haud yer gab or they'll hae ye oot."

Bobby dropped like a shot, cringing at Auld Jock's feet. The most sensitive of four-footed creatures in the world, the Skye terrier is utterly abased by a rebuke from his master. The whole garret was soon in an uproar of vile accusation and shrill denial that spread from cell to cell. Auld Jock glowered down at Bobby with frightened eyes. In the winters he had lodged there he had lived unmolested only because he had managed to escape notice. Timid old country body that he was, he could not "fecht it oot" with the thieves and beggars and drunkards of the Cowgate. By and by the brawling died down. In the double row of little dens this one alone was silent, and the offending dog was not located.

But when the danger was past, Auld Jock's heart was pounding in his chest. His legs gave way under him, when he got up to fetch the candle from near the door and set it on a projecting brick in the fireplace. By its light he began to read in a small pocket Bible the Psalm that had always fascinated him because he had never been able to understand it.

"The Lord is my Shepherd; I shall not want." So far it was plain and comforting. "He maketh me to lie down in green pastures. He leadeth me beside the still waters."

Nae, the pastures were brown, or purple and yellow with heather and gorse. Rocks cropped out everywhere, and the peaty tarns were mostly bleak and frozen. The broad Firth was ever ebbing and flowing with the restless sea, and the burns bickering down the glens. The minister of the little hill kirk had said once that in England the pastures were green and the lakes still and bright; but that was a fey, foreign country to which Auld Jock had no desire to go. He wondered, wistfully, if he would feel at hame in God's heaven, and if there would be room in that lush silence for a noisy little dog, as there was on the rough Pentland braes. And there his thoughts came back to this cold prison cell in which he could not defend the right of his one faithful little friend to live. He stooped and lifted Bobby into the bed. Humble, and eager to be forgiven for an offense he could not understand, the loving little creature leaped to Auld Jock's arms and lavished frantic endearments upon him.

Lying so together in the dark, man and dog fell into a sleep that was broken by Auld Jock's fitful coughing and the abuse of his neighbors. It was not until the wind had long died to a muffled murmur at the casements, and every other lodger was out, that Auld Jock slept soundly. He awoke late to find Bobby waiting patiently on the floor and the bare cell flooded with white glory. That could mean but one thing. He stumbled dizzily to his feet and threw a sash back. Over the huddle of high housetops, the University towers and the scattered suburbs beyond, he looked away to the snow-clad slopes of the Pentlands, running up to heaven and shining under the pale winter sunshine.

"The snaw! Eh, Bobby, but it's a bonny sicht to auld een!" he cried, with the simple delight of a child. He stooped to lift Bobby to the wonder of it, when the world suddenly went black and roaring around in his head. Staggering back he crumpled up in a pitiful heap on the floor.

Bobby licked his master's face and hands, and then sat quietly down beside him. So many strange, uncanny things had happened within the last twenty-four hours that the little dog was rapidly outgrowing his irresponsible puppyhood. After a long time Auld Jock opened his eyes and sat up. Bobby put his paws on his master's knees in anxious sympathy. Before the man had got his wits about him the time-gun boomed from the Castle. Panic-stricken that he should have slept in his bed so late, and then lain senseless on the floor for he knew not how long, Auld Jock got up and struggled into his greatcoat, bonnet and plaid. In feeling for his woolen mittens he discovered the buns that Mr. Traill had dropped into his pocket for Bobby.

The old man stared and stared at them in piteous dismay. Mr. Traill had believed him to be so ill that he "wouldna be oot the morn." It was a staggering thought.

The bells of St. Giles broke into "Over the Hills and Far Away." The melody came to Auld Jock clearly, unbroken by echoes, for the garret was on a level with the cathedral's crown on High Street. It brought to him again a vision of the Midlothian slopes, but it reminded Bobby that it was dinner-time. He told Auld Jock so by running to the door and back and begging him, by every pretty wile at his command, to go. The old man got to his feet and then fell back, pale and shaken, his heart hammering again. Bobby ate the bun soberly and then sat up against Auld Jock's feet, that dangled helplessly from the bed. The bells died away from the man's ears before they had ceased playing. Both the church and the University bells struck the hour of two—then three—then four. Daylight had begun to fail when Auld Jock stirred, sat up, and did a strange thing: taking from his pocket a leather bag-purse that was closed by a draw-string, he counted the few crowns and shillings in it and the many smaller silver and copper coins.

GREYFRIARS BOBBY

"There's eneugh," he said. There was enough, by careful spending, to pay for food and lodging for a few weeks, to save himself from the charity of the infirmary. By this act he admitted the humiliating and fearful fact that he was very ill. The precious little hoard must be hidden from the chance prowler. He looked for a loose brick in the fireplace, but before he found one he forgot all about it, and absent - mindedly heaped the coins in a little pile on the open Bible at the back of the bed.

For a long time Auld Jock sat there with his head in his hands before he again slipped back to his pillow. Darkness stole into the quiet room. The lodgers returned to their dens one after one, tramping or slipping or hobbling up the stairs and along the passage. Bobby bristled and froze, on guard, when a stealthy hand tried the latch. Then there were sounds of fighting, of crying women, and the long, low wailing of wretched children. The evening drum and bugle were heard from the Castle, and hour after hour was struck from the clock of St. Giles while Bobby watched beside his master.

All night Auld Jock was "aff 'is heid." When he muttered in his sleep or cried out in the delirium of fever, the little dog put his paws upon the bed-rail. He scratched on it and begged to be lifted to where he could comfort his master, for the shelf was set too high for him to climb into the bed. Unable to get his master's attention, he licked the hot hand that hung over the side. Auld Jock lay still at last, not coughing any more, but breathing rapid, shallow breaths. Just at dawn he turned his head and gazed in bewilderment at the alert and troubled little creature that was instantly upon the rail. After a long time he recognized the dog and patted the shaggy little head. Feeling around the bed, he found the other bun and dropped it on the floor. Presently he said, between strangled breaths:

"Puir — Bobby! Gang — awa' — hame — laddie."

After that it was suddenly very still in the brightening room. Bobby gazed and gazed at his master — one long, heartbroken look, then dropped to all fours and stood trembling. Without another look he stretched himself upon the hearthstone below the bed.

Morning and evening footsteps went down and came up on the stairs. Throughout the day—the babel of crowded tenement strife; the crying of fishwives and fagot-venders in the court; the striking of the hours; the boom of the time-gun and sweet clamor of music bells; the failing of

the light and the soaring note of the bugle—
Bobby watched motionless beside his master.

Very late at night shuffling footsteps came
up the stairs. The "auld wifie" kept a sharp eye
on the comings and goings of her lodgers. It
was " no' canny" that this old man, with a cauld
in his chest, had gone up full two days before and
had not come down again. To bitter complaints
of his coughing and of his strange talking to himself she gave scant attention, but foul play
was done often enough in these dens to make her
uneasy. She had no desire to have the Burgh
police coming about and interfering with her
business. She knocked sharply on the door and
called:

"Auld Jock!"

Bobby trotted over to the door and stood
looking at it. In such a strait he would naturally have welcomed the visitor, scratching on the
panel, and crying to any human body without
to come in and see what had befallen his master.
But Auld Jock had bade him "haud 'is gab"
there, as in Greyfriars kirkyard. So he held to
loyal silence, although the knocking and shaking
of the latch was insistent and the lodgers were
astir. The voice of the old woman was shrill
with alarm.

"Auld Jock, can ye no' wauken?" And, after

a moment, in which the unlatched casement window within could be heard creaking on its hinges in the chill breeze, there was a hushed and frightened question:

"Are ye deid?"

The footsteps fled down the stairs, and Bobby was left to watch through the long hours of darkness.

Very early in the morning the flimsy door was quietly forced by authority. The first man who entered—an officer of the Crown from the sheriff's court on the bridge — took off his hat to the majesty that dominated that bare cell. The Cowgate region presented many a startling contrast, but such a one as this must seldom have been seen. The classic fireplace, and the motionless figure and peaceful face of the pious old shepherd within it, had the dignity and beauty of some monumental tomb and carven effigy in old Greyfriars kirkyard. Only less strange was the contrast between the marks of poverty and toil on the dead man and the dainty grace of the little fluff of a dog that mourned him.

No such men as these—officers of her Majesty the Queen, Burgh policemen, and learned doctors from the Royal Infirmary—had ever been aware of Auld Jock, living. Dead, and no' needing them any more, they stood guard over him

and inquired sternly as to the manner in which
he had died. There was a hysterical breath of
relief from the crowd of lodgers and tenants when
the little pile of coins was found on the Bible.
There had been no foul play. Auld Jock had
died of heart failure, from pneumonia and worn-
out old age.

"There's eneugh," a Burgh policeman said
when the money was counted. He meant much
the same thing Auld Jock himself had meant.
There was enough to save him from the last
indignity a life of useful labor can thrust upon
the honest poor—pauper burial. But when inquiries were made for the name and the friends
of this old man there appeared to be only "Auld
Jock" to enter into the record, and a little dog
to follow the body to the grave. It was a Bible-
reader who chanced to come in from the Medical
Mission in the Cowgate who thought to look in
the fly-leaf of Auld Jock's Bible.

"His name is John Gray."

He laid the worn little book on Auld Jock's
breast and crossed the work-scarred hands upon
it. "It's something by the ordinar' to find a gude
auld country body in such a foul place." He
stooped and patted Bobby, and noted the bun, un-
touched, upon the floor. Turning to a wild elf of
a barefooted child in the crowd he spoke to her.

"Would you share your gude brose with the bit dog, lassie?"

She darted down the stairs, and presently returned with her own scanty bowl of breakfast porridge. Bobby refused the food, but he looked at her so mournfully that the first tears of pity her unchildlike eyes had ever shed welled up. She put out her hand timidly and stroked him.

It was just before the report of the time-gun that two policemen cleared the stairs, shrouded Auld Jock in his own greatcoat and plaid, and carried him down to the court. There they laid him in a plain box of white deal that stood on the pavement, closed it, and went away down the wynd on a necessary errand. The Bible-reader sat on an empty beer keg to guard the box, and Bobby climbed on the top and stretched himself above his master. The court was a well, more than a hundred feet deep. What sky might have been visible above it was hidden by tier above tier of dingy, tattered washings. The stairway filled again, and throngs of outcasts of every sort went about their squalid businesses, with only a curious glance or so at the pathetic group.

Presently the policemen returned from the Cowgate with a motley assortment of pall-bearers. There was a good-tempered Irish laborer from a near-by brewery; a decayed gentleman, unsteady of gait and blear-eyed, in a greasy frock-coat and broken hat; a flashily dressed bartender who found the task distasteful; a stout, bent-backed fagot-carrier; a drunken fisherman from New Haven, suddenly sobered by this uncanny duty, and a furtive-eyed, gaol-bleached thief who feared a trap and tried to escape.

Tailed by scuffling gamins, the strange little procession moved quickly down the wynd and turned into the roaring Cowgate. The policemen went before to force a passage through the press. The Bible-reader followed the box, and Bobby, head and tail down, trotted unnoticed, beneath it. The humble funeral train passed under a bridge arch into the empty Grassmarket, and went up Candlemakers Row to the kirkyard gate. Such as Auld Jock, now, by unnumbered thousands, were coming to lie among the grand and great, laird and leddy, poet and prophet, persecutor and martyr, in the piled-up, historic burying-ground of old Greyfriars.

By a gesture the caretaker directed the bearers to the right, past the church, and on down the crowded slope to the north, that was circled about by the backs of the tenements in the Grassmarket and Candlemakers Row. The boy

GREYFRIARS BOBBY

was lowered at once, and the pall-bearers hastily departed to delayed dinners. The policemen had urgent duties elsewhere. Only the Bible-reader remained to see the grave partly filled in, and to try to persuade Bobby to go away with him. But the little dog resisted with such piteous struggles that the man put him down again. The grave-digger leaned on his spade for a bit of professional talk.

"Mony a dog gangs daft an' greets like a human body when his maister dees. They're aye put oot, a time or twa, an' they gang to folk that ken them, an' syne they tak' to ithers. Dinna fash yersel' aboot 'im. He wullna greet lang."

Since Bobby would not go, there was nothing to do but leave him there; but it was with many a backward look and disturbing doubt that the good man turned away. The grave-digger finished his task cheerfully, shouldered his tools, and left the kirkyard. The early dark was coming on when the caretaker, in making his last rounds, found the little terrier flattened out on the new-made mound.

"Gang awa' oot!" he ordered. Bobby looked up pleadingly and trembled, but he made no motion to obey. James Brown was not an unfeeling man, and he was but doing his duty. From an impulse of pity for this bonny wee bit of loyalty

60

and grief he picked Bobby up, carried him all the way to the gate and set him over the wicket on the pavement.

"Gang awa' hame, noo," he said, kindly. "A kirkya'rd isna a place for a bit dog to be leevin'."

Bobby lay where he had been dropped until the caretaker was out of sight. Then, finding the aperture under the gate too small for him to squeeze through, he tried, in his ancestral way, to enlarge it by digging. He scratched and scratched at the unyielding stone until his little claws were broken and his toes bleeding, before he stopped and lay down with his nose under the wicket.

Just before the closing hour a carriage stopped at the kirkyard gate. A black-robed lady, carrying flowers, hurried through the wicket. Bobby slipped in behind her and disappeared.

After nightfall, when the lamps were lighted on the bridge, when Mr. Traill had come out to stand idly in his doorway, looking for some one to talk to, and James Brown had locked the kirk-yard gate for the night and gone into his little stone lodge to supper, Bobby came out of hiding and stretched himself prone across Auld Jock's grave.

IV

FIFTEEN minutes after the report of the time-gun on Monday, when the bells were playing their merriest and the dining-rooms were busiest, Mr. Traill felt such a tiny tug at his trouser-leg that it was repeated before he gave it attention. In the press of hungry guests Bobby had little more than room to rise in his pretty, begging attitude. The landlord was so relieved to see him again, after five conscience-stricken days, that he stooped to clap the little dog on the side and to greet him with jocose approval.

"Gude dog to fetch Auld Jock—"

With a faint and piteous cry that was heard by no one but Mr. Traill, Bobby toppled over on the floor. It was a limp little bundle that the land-lord picked up from under foot and held on his arm a moment, while he looked around for the dog's master. Shocked at not seeing Auld Jock, by a kind of inspiration he carried the little dog to the inglenook and laid him down under the familiar settle. Bobby was little more than

62

breathing, but he opened his silkily veiled brown eyes and licked the friendly hand that had done him this refinement of kindness. It took Mr. Traill more than a moment to realize the nature of the trouble. A dog with so thick a fleece of wool, under so crisply waving an outer coat as Bobby's, may perish for lack of food and show no outward sign of emaciation.

"The sonsie, wee—why, he's all but starved!"

Pale with pity, Mr. Traill snatched a plate of broth from the hands of a gaping waiter laddie, set it under Bobby's nose, and watched him begin to lap the warm liquid eagerly. In the busy place the incident passed unnoticed. With his usual, brisk decision Mr. Traill turned the backs of a couple of chairs over against the nearest table, to signify that the corner was reserved, and he went about his duties with unwonted silence. As the crowd thinned he returned to the inglenook to find Bobby asleep, not curled up in a tousled ball, as such a little dog should be, but stretched on his side and breathing irregularly.

If Bobby was in such straits, how must it be with Auld Jock? This was the fifth day since the sick old man had fled into the storm. With new disquiet Mr. Traill remembered a matter that had annoyed him in the morning, and that he had been inclined to charge to mischievous Heriot boys. Low down on the outside of his freshly varnished entrance door were many scratches that Bobby could have made. He may have come for food on the Sabbath day when the place was closed.

After an hour Bobby woke long enough to eat a generous plate of that delectable and highly nourishing Scotch dish known as haggis. He fell asleep again in an easier attitude that relieved the tension on the landlord's feelings. Confident that the devoted little dog would lead him straight to his master, Mr. Traill closed the door securely, that he might not escape unnoticed, and arranged his own worldly affairs so he could leave them to hirelings on the instant. In the idle time between dinner and supper he sat down by the fire, lighted his pipe, repented his unruly tongue, and waited. As the short day darkened to its close the sunset bugle was blown in the Castle. At the first note Bobby crept from under the settle, a little unsteady on his legs as yet, wagged his tail for thanks, and trotted to the door.

Mr. Traill had no trouble at all in keeping the little dog in sight to the kirkyard gate, for in the dusk his coat shone silvery white. Indeed, by a backward look now and then, Bobby seemed to invite the man to follow, and waited at the

gate, with some impatience, for him to come
up. Help was needed there. By rising and
tugging at Mr. Traill's clothing and then jumping
on the wicket Bobby plainly begged to have it
opened. He made no noise, neither barking nor
whimpering and that was very strange for a
dog of the terrier breed; but each instant of
delay he became more insistent, and even frantic, to have the gate unlatched. Mr. Traill refused to believe what Bobby's behavior indicated,
and rep oved him in the broad Scotch to which
the country dog was used.

"Nae, Bobby; be a gude dog. Gang doon to
the Coogate noo, an' find Auld Jock."

Uttering no cry at all, Bobby gave the man
such a woebegone look and dropped to the pavement, with his long muzzle as far under the
wicket as he could thrust it, that the truth shot
home to Mr. Traill's understanding. He opened
the gate. Bobby slipped through and stood just
inside a moment, and looking back as if he expected his human friend to follow. Then, very
suddenly, as the door of the lodge opened and the
caretaker came out, Bobby disappeared in the
shadow of the church.

A big-boned, slow-moving man of the best
country-house-gardener type, serviceably dressed
in corduroy, wool bonnet, and ribbed stockings,

James Brown collided with the small and **wiry** landlord, to his own very great embarrassment.

"Eh, Maister Traill, ye gied me a turn. It's no' canny to be proolin' aboot the kirkyaird i' the gloamin'."

"Whaur did the bit dog go, man?" demanded the peremptory landlord.

"Dog? There's no' ony dog i' the kirkyaird. It isna permeetted. Gin it's a pussy ye're needin', noo—"

But Mr. Traill brushed this irrelevant pleasantry aside.

"Ay, there's a dog. I let him in my ainsel'."

The caretaker exploded with wrath: "Syne I'll hae the law on ye. Can ye no' read, man?"

"Tut, tut, Jeemes Brown. Don't stand there arguing. It's a gude and necessary regulation, but it's no' the law o' the land. I turned the dog in to settle a matter with my ain conscience, and John Knox would have done the same thing in the bonny face o' Queen Mary. What it is, is nae beesiness of yours. The dog was a sma' young terrier of the Highland breed, but with a drop to his ears and a crinkle in his frosty coat— no' just an ordinar' dog. I know him weel. He came to my place to be fed, near dead of hunger, then led me here. If his master lies in this kirkyard I'll tak' the bit dog awa' with me."

Mr. Traill's astonishing fluency always carried all walls of resistance before it with men of slower wit and speech. Only a superior man could brush time-honored rules aside so curtly and stand on his human rights so surely. James Brown pulled his bonnet off deferentially, scratched his shock head and shifted his pipe. Finally he admitted:

"Weel, there was a bit tyke i' the kirkyaird twa days syne. I put 'im oot, an' haena seen 'im aboot ony mair." He offered, however, to show the new-made mound on which he had found the dog. Leading the way past the church, he went on down the terraced slope, prolonging the walk with conversation, for the guardianship of an old churchyard offers very little such lively company as John Traill's.

"I mind, noo, it was some puir body frae the Coogate, wi' no' ony mourners but the sma' terrier aneath the coffin. I let 'im pass, no' to mak' a disturbance at a buryin'. The deal box was fetched up by the police, an' carried by sic a crew o' gaol-birds as wad mak' ye turn ower in yer ain God's hole. But he paid for his buryin' wi' his ain siller, an' noo lies as canny as the nobeelity, nae doot. Here's the place, Maister Traill; an' ye can see for yer ainsel' there's no' ony dog."

"Ay, that would be Auld Jock and Bobby would no' be leaving him," insisted the landlord, stubbornly. He stood looking down at the rough mound of frozen clods heaped in a little space of trampled snow.

"Jeemes Brown," Mr. Trail said, at last, "the man wha lies here was a decent, pious auld country body, and I drove him to his meeserable death in the Cowgate."

"Man, ye dinna ken what ye're sayin'!" was the shocked response.

"Do I no'? I'm canny, by the ordinar', but my fule tongue will get me into trouble with the magistrates one of these days. It aye wags at both ends, and is no' tied in the middle."

Then, stanch Calvinist that he was, and never dreaming that he was indulging in the sinful pleasure of confession, Mr. Traill poured out the story of Auld Jock's plight and of his own shortcomings. It was a bitter, upbraiding thing that he, an uncommonly capable man, had meant so well by a humble old body, and done so ill. And he had failed again when he tried to undo the mischief. The very next morning he had gone down into the perilous Cowgate, and inquired in every place where it might be possible for such a timid old shepherd to be known. But there! As well look for a burr thistle in a

bin of oats, as look for a human atom in the Cowgate and the wynds "juist aff."

"Weel, noo, ye couldna hae dune aething wi'
the auld body, ava, gin he wouldna gang to the
infairmary." The caretaker was trying to console the self-accusing man.

"Could I no'? Ye dinna ken me as weel as
ye micht." The disgusted landlord tumbled
into broad Scotch. "Gie me to do it ance mair,
an' I'd chairge Auld Jock wi' thievin' ma siller,
wi' a wink o' the ee at the police to mak' them
ken I was leein'; an' syne they'd hae hustled 'im
aff, willy-nilly, to a snug bed."

The energetic little man looked so entirely
capable of any daring deed that he fired the
caretaker into enthusiastic search for Bobby.
It was not entirely dark, for the sky was studded
with stars, snow lay in broad patches on the
slope, and all about the lower end of the kirkyard
supper candles burned at every rear window of
the tall tenements.

The two men searched among the near-by slabs
and table-tombs and scattered thorn bushes.
They circled the monument to all the martyrs
who had died heroically, in the Grassmarket and
elsewhere, for their faith. They hunted in the
deep shadows of the buttresses along the side of
the auld kirk and among the pillars of the octag

onal portico to the new. At the rear of the long, low building, that was clumsily partitioned across for two pulpits, stood the ornate tomb of "Bluidy" McKenzie. But Bobby had not committed himself to the mercy of the hanging judge, nor yet to the care of the doughty minister, who, from the pulpit of Greyfriars auld kirk, had flung the blood and tear stained Covenant in the teeth of persecution.

The search was continued past the modest Scott family burial plot and on to the west wall. There was a broad outlook over Heriot's Hospital grounds, a smooth and shining expanse of unsullied snow about the early Elizabethan pile of buildings. Returning, they skirted the lowest wall below the tenements, for in the circling line of courtyarded vaults, where the "nobeelity" of Scotland lay haughtily apart under time-stained marbles, were many shadowy nooks in which so small a dog could stow himself away. Skulking cats were flushed there, and sent flying over aristocratic bones, but there was no trace of Bobby.

The second tier of windows of the tenements was level with the kirkyard wall, and several times Mr. Traill called up to a lighted casement where a family sat at a scant supper:

"Have you seen a bit dog, man?"

There was much cordial interest in his quest, windows opening and faces staring into the dusk; but not until near the top of the Row was a clue gained. Then, at the query, an unkempt, ill-clad lassie slipped from her stool and leaned out over the pediment of a tomb. She had seen a "wee, wee doggie jinkin' amang the stanes." It was on the Sabbath evening, when the well-dressed folk had gone home from the afternoon services. She was eating her porridge at the window, "by her lane," when he "keeked up at her so knowing, and begged so bonny," that she balanced her bit bowl on a lath, and pushed it over on the kirkyard wall. As she finished the story the big, blue eyes of the little maid, who doubtless had herself known what it was to be hungry, filled with tears.

"The wee tyke couldna loup up to it, an' a deil o' a pussy got it a'. He was so bonny, like a leddy's pet, an' syne he fell ower on the snaw an' creepit awa'. He didna cry oot, but he was a' but deid wi' hunger." At the memory of it soft-hearted Ailie Lindsey sobbed on her mother's shoulder.

The tale was retold from one excited window to another, all the way around and all the way up to the gables, so quickly could some incident of human interest make a social gathering in the populous tenements. Most of all, the children seized upon the touching story. Eager and pinched little faces peered wistfully into the melancholy kirkyard.

"Is he yer ain dog?" crippled Tammy Barr piped out, in his thin treble. "Gin I had a bonny wee dog I'd gie 'im ma ain brose, an' cuddle 'im, an' he couldna gang awa'."

"Nae, laddie, he's no' my dog. His master lies buried here, and the leal Highlander mourns for him." With keener appreciation of its pathos Mr. Traill recalled that this was what Auld Jock had said: "Bobby isna ma ain dog." And he was conscious of wishing that Bobby was his own, with his unpurchasable love and a loyalty to face starvation. As he mounted the turfed terraces he thought to call back:

"If you see him again, lassie, call him 'Bobby,' and fetch him up to Greyfriars Dining-Rooms. I have a bright siller shulling, with the Queen's bonny face on it, to give the bairn that finds Bobby."

There was excited comment on this. He must, indeed, be an attractive dog to be worth a shulling. The children generously shared plans for capturing Bobby. But presently the windows were closed, and supper was resumed. The caretaker was irritable.

"Noo, ye'll hae them a' oot swarmin' ower the kirkyaird. There's nae coontin' the bairns o' the neeborhood, an' nane o' them are so weel broucht up as they micht be."

Mr. Traill commented upon this philosophically: "A bairn is like a dog in mony ways. Tak' a stick to one or the other and he'll misbehave. The children here are poor and neglected, but they're no' vicious like the awfu' imps of the Cowgate, wha'd steal from their blind grandmithers. Get on the gude side of the bairns, man, and you'll live easier and die happier."

It seemed useless to search the much longer arm of the kirkyard that ran southward behind the shops of Greyfriars Place and Forest Road. If Bobby was in the inclosure at all he would not be far from Auld Jock's grave. Nearest the new-made mound were two very old and dark table-tombs. The farther one lay horizontally, on its upright "through stanes," some distance above the earth. The supports of the other had fallen, and the table lay on their thickness within six inches of the ground. Mr. Traill and the caretaker sat upon this slab, which testified to the piety and worth of one Mistress Jean Grant, who had died "lang syne."

Encroached upon, as it was, by unlovely life,

GREYFRIARS BOBBY

Greyfriars kirkyard was yet a place of solitude and peace. The building had the dignity that only old age can give. It had lost its tower by an explosion of gunpowder stored there in war time, and its walls and many of the ancient tombs bore the marks of fire and shot. Within the last decade some of the Gothic openings had been filled with beautiful memorial windows. Despite the horrors and absurdities and mutilation of much of the funeral sculpturing, the kirkyard had a sad distinction, such as became its fame as Scotland's Westminster. And there was one heavenward outlook and heavenly view. Over the tallest decaying tenement one could look up to the Castle of dreams on the crag, and drop the glance all the way down the pinnacled crest of High Street, to the dark and deserted Palace of Holyrood. After nightfall the turreted heights wore a luminous crown, and the steep ridge up to it twinkled with myriad lights. After a time the caretaker offered a well-considered opinion.

"The dog maun hae left the kirkyaird. Thae terriers are aye barkin'. It'd be maist michty noo, gin he'd be so lang i' the kirkyaird, an' no' mak' a blatterin'."

As a man of superior knowledge Mr. Traill found pleasure in upsetting this theory. "The

Highland breed are no' like ordinar' terriers.
Noisy enough to deave one, by nature, give a bit
Skye a reason and he'll lie a' the day under a
whin bush on the brae, as canny as a fox. You
gave Bobby a reason for hiding here by turning
him out. And Auld Jock was a vera releegious
man. It would no' be surprising if he taught
Bobby to hold his tongue in a kirkyard."

"Man, he did that vera thing." James
Brown brought his fist down on his knee; for
suddenly he identified Bobby as the snappy little
ruffian that had chased the cat and bitten his
shins, and Auld Jock as the scandalized shepherd
who had rebuked the dog so bitterly. He related the incident with gusto.

"The auld man cried oot on the misbehavin'
tyke to haud 'is gab. Syne, ye ne'er saw the
bit dog's like for a bairn that'd haen a lickin'.
He'd 'a' gaen into a pit, gin there'd been ane, an'
pu'd it in ahind 'im. I turned 'em baith oot, an'
told 'em no' to come back. Eh, man, it's fearsome hoo ilka body comes to a kirkyaird, toes
afore 'im, in a long box."

Mr. Brown was sobered by this grim thought
and then, in his turn, he confessed a slip to this
tolerant man of the world. "The wee deil o' a
sperity dog nipped me so I let oot an aith."

"Ay, that's Bobby. He would no' be afraid

of onything with hide or hair on it. Man, the
Skye terriers go into dens of foxes and wildcats,
and worry bulls till they tak' to their heels.
And Bobby's sagacious by the ordinar'." He
thought intently for a moment, and then spoke
naturally, and much as Auld Jock himself might
have spoken to the dog.

"Whaur are ye, Bobby? Come awa' oot,
laddie!"

Instantly the little dog stood before him like
some conjured ghost. He had slipped from
under the slab on which they were sitting. It
lay so near the ground, and in such a mat of
dead grass, that it had not occurred to them to
look for him there. He came up to Mr. Traill
confidingly, submitted to having his head patted,
and looked pleadingly at the caretaker. Then,
thinking he had permission to do so, he lay down
on the mound. James Brown dropped his pipe.

"It's maist michty!" he said.

Mr. Traill got to his feet briskly. "I'll just
tak' the dog with me, Mr. Brown. On market-
day I'll find the farmer that owns him and send
him hame. As you say, a kirkyard's nae place
for a dog to be living neglected. Come awa',
Bobby."

Bobby looked up, but, as he made no motion
to obey, Mr. Traill stooped and lifted him

From sheer surprise at this unexpected move **the** little dog lay still a moment on the man's arm. Then, with a lithe twist of his muscular body and a spring, he was on the ground, trembling, re- proachful for the breach of faith, but braced for resistance.

"Eh, you're no' going?" Mr. Traill put his hands in his pockets, looked down at Bobby ad- miringly, and sighed. "There's a dog after my ain heart, and he'll have naething to do with me. He has a mind of his ain. I'll just have to be leaving him here the two days, Mr. Brown."

"Ye wullna leave 'im! Ye'll tak' 'im wi' ye, or I'll hae to put 'im oot. Man, I couldna haud the place gin I brak the rules."

"You — will — no' — put — the — wee — dog — out!" Mr. Traill shook a playful, emphatic finger under the big man's nose.

"Why wull I no'?"

"Because, man, you have a vera soft heart, and you canna deny it." It was with a genial, confident smile that Mr. Traill made this terrible accusation.

"Ma heart's no' so saft as to permit a bit dog to scandalize the deid."

"He's been here two days, you no' knowing it, and he has scandalized neither the dead nor the living. He's as leal as ony Covenanter here, and

better conducted than mony a laird. He's no
the quarrelsome kind, but, man, for a preenciple
he'd fight like auld Clootie." Here the landlord's heat gave way to pure enjoyment of the
situation. "Eh, I'd like to see you put him out.
It would be another Flodden Field."

The angry caretaker shrugged his broad
shoulders.

"Ye can see it, gin ye stand by, in juist ane
meenit. Fecht as he may, it wull soon be ower."

Mr. Traill laughed easily, and ventured the
opinion that Mr. Brown's bark was worse than
his bite. As he went through the gateway he
could not resist calling back a challenge: "I
daur you to do it."

Mr. Brown locked the gate, went sulkily into
the lodge, lighted his cutty pipe, and smoked it
furiously. He read a Psalm with deliberation,
poked up an already bright fire, and glowered at
his placid gude wife. It was not to be borne—
to be defied by a ten-inch-high terrier, and dared,
by a man a third under his own weight, to do his
duty. After an hour or so he worked himself
up to the point of going out and slamming the
door.

At eight o'clock Mr. Traill found Bobby on the
pavement outside the locked gate. He was not
sorry that the fortunes of unequal battle had

thrown the faithful little dog on his hospitality.
Bobby begged piteously to be put inside, but he
seemed to understand at last that the gate
was too high for Mr. Traill to drop him over.
He followed the landlord up to the restaurant
willingly. He may have thought this champion
had another solution of the difficulty, for when
he saw the man settle comfortably in a chair he
refused to lie on the hearth. He ran to the door
and back, and begged and whined to be let out.
For a long time he stood dejectedly. He was
not sullen, for he ate a light supper and thanked
his host with much polite wagging, and he even
allowed himself to be petted. Suddenly he
thought of something, trotted briskly off to a
corner and crouched there.

Mr. Traill watched the attractive little creature
with interest and growing affection. Very likely
he indulged in a day-dream that, perhaps, the
tenant of Cauldbrae farm could be induced to
part with Bobby for a consideration, and that he
himself could win the dog to transfer his love
from a cold grave to a warm hearth.

With a spring the rat was captured. A jerk
of the long head and there was proof of Bobby's
prowess to lay at his good friend's feet. Made
much of, and in a position to ask fresh favors,
the little dog was off to the door with cheerful,

staccato barks. His reasoning was as plain as print: "I hae done ye a service, noo tak' me back to the kirkyaird."

Mr. Traill talked to him as he might have reasoned with a bright bairn. Bobby listened patiently, but remained of the same mind. At last he moved away, disappointed in this human person, discouraged, but undefeated in his purpose. He lay down by the door. Mr. Traill watched him, for if any chance late comer opened the door the masterless little dog would be out into the perils of the street. Bobby knew what doors were for and, very likely, expected some such release. He waited a long time patiently. Then he began to run back and forth. He put his paws upon Mr. Traill and whimpered and cried. Finally he howled.

It was a dreadful, dismal, heartbroken howl that echoed back from the walls. He howled continuously, until the landlord, quite distracted, and concerned about the peace of his neighbors, thrust Bobby into the dark scullery at the rear, and bade him stop his noise. For fully ten minutes the dog was quiet. He was probably engaged in exploring his new quarters to find an outlet. Then he began to howl again. It was truly astonishing that so small a dog could make so large a noise.

GREYFRIARS BOBBY

A battle was on between the endurance of the man and the persistence of the terrier. Mr. Traill was speculating on which was likely to be victor in the contest, when the front door was opened and the proprietor of the Book Hunter's Stall put in a bare, bald head and the abstracted face of the book-worm that is mildly amused.

"Have you tak'n to a dog at your time o' life, Mr. Traill?"

"Ay, man, and it would be all right if the bit dog would just tak' to me."

This pleasantry annoyed a good man who had small sense of humor, and he remarked testily· "The barkin' disturbs my customers so they canna read." The place was a resort for student laddies who had to be saving of candles.

"That's no right," the landlord admitted, sympathetically. "'Reading mak'th a full man.' Eh, what a deeference to the warld if Robbie Burns had aye preferred a book to a bottle." The bookseller refused to be beguiled from his just cause of complaint into the flowery meads of literary reminiscences and speculations.

"You'll stop that dog's deaving noise, Mr. Traill, or I'll appeal to the Burgh police."

The landlord returned a bland and child-like smile. "You'd be weel within your legal rights to do it, neebor."

The door was shut with such a business - like click that the situation suddenly became serious. Bobby's vocal powers, however, gave no signs of diminishing. Mr. Traill quieted the dog for a few moments by letting him into the outer room, but the swiftness and energy with which he renewed his attacks on the door, and on the man's will, showed plainly that the truce was only temporary. He did not know what he meant to do except that he certainly had no intention of abandoning the little dog. To gain time he put on his hat and coat, picked Bobby up, and opened the door. The thought occurred to him to try the gate at the upper end of the kirkyard or, that failing, to get into Heriot's Hospital grounds and put Bobby over the wall. As he opened the door, however, he heard Geordie Ross's whistle around the bend in Forest Road.

"Hey, laddie!" he called. "Come awa' in a meenit." When the sturdy boy was inside, and the door safely shut, he began in his most guileless and persuasive tone: "Would you like to earn a shulling, Geordie?"

"Ay, I would. Gie it to me i' pennies an' ha'pennies, Maister Traill. It seems mair, an' mak's a braw jinglin' in a pocket."

The price was paid and the tale told. The quick championship of the boy was engaged for the gallant dog, and Geordie's eyes sparkled at the prospect of dark adventure. Bobby was on the floor listening, ears and eyes, brambly muzzle and feathered tail alert. He listened with his whole, small, excited body, and hung on the answer to the momentous question.

"Is there no a way to smuggle the bit dog into the kirkyard?"

It appeared that nothing was easier, "aince ye ken hoo." Did Mr. Traill know of the internal highway through the old Cunzie Neuk at the bottom of the Row? One went up the stairs on the front to the low, timbered gallery, then through a passage as black as "Bluidy" McKenzie's heart. At the end of that one came to a peep-hole of a window, set out on wooden brackets, that hung right over the kirkyard wall. From that window Bobby could be dropped on a certain noble vault, from which he could jump to the ground.

"Twa meenits' wark, stout hearts, sleekit footstaps, an' the fearsome deed is done," declared twelve - year - old Geordie, whose sense of the dramatic matched his daring.

But when the deed was done, and the two stood innocently on the brightly lighted approach to the bridge, Mr. Traill had his misgivings. A well-respected business man and church-member.

he felt uneasy to be at the mercy of a laddie who might be boastful.

"Geordie, if you tell onybody about this I'll have to give you a licking."

"I wullna tell," Geordie reassured him. "It's no' so respectable, an' syne ma mither'd gie me anither lickin', an' they'd gie me twa more awfu' anes, an' black marks for a month, at Heriot's."

V

WORD had been left at all the inns and carting offices about both markets for the tenant of Cauldbrae farm to call at Mr. Traill's place for Bobby. The man appeared Wednesday afternoon, driving a big Clydesdale horse to a stout farm cart. The low-ceiled dining-room suddenly shrank about the big-boned, long-legged hill man. The fact embarrassed him, as did also a voice cultivated out of all proportion to town houses, by shouting to dogs and shepherds on windy shoulders of the Pentlands.

"Hae ye got the dog wi' ye?"

Mr. Traill pointed to Bobby, deep in a blissful, after-dinner nap under the settle.

The farmer breathed a sigh of relief, sat at a table, and ate a frugal meal of bread and cheese. As roughly dressed as Auld Jock, in a metal-buttoned greatcoat of hodden gray, a woolen bonnet, and the shepherd's twofold plaid, he was a different species of human being altogether. A long, lean, sinewy man of early middle age, he had a smooth-shaven, bony jaw, far-seeing gray eyes under furzy brows, and a shock of auburn hair. When he spoke, it was to give bits out of his own experience.

"Thae terriers are usefu' eneugh on an ordinar' fairm an' i' the toon to keep awa' the vermin, but I wadna gie a twa-penny-bit for ane o' them on a sheep-fairm. There's a wee lassie at Cauldbrae wha wants Bobby for a pet. It wasna richt for Auld Jock to win 'im awa' frae the bairn."

Mr. Traill's hand was lifted in rebuke. "Speak nae ill, man; Auld Jock's dead."

The farmer's ruddy face blanched and he dropped his knife. "He's no' buried so sune?"

"Ay, he's buried four days since in Greyfriars kirkyard, and Bobby has slept every night on the auld man's grave."

"I'll juist tak' a leuk at the grave, mon, gin ye'll hae an ee on the dog."

Mr. Traill cautioned him not to let the caretaker know that Bobby had continued to sleep in the kirkyard, after having been put out twice. The farmer was back in ten minutes, with a canny face that defied reading. He lighted his short Dublin pipe and smoked it out before he spoke again.

"It's ower grand for a puir auld shepherd body to be buried i' Greyfriars."

"No' so grand as heaven, I'm thinking."
Mr. Traill's response was dry.

"Ay, an' we're a' coontin' on gangin' there;
but it's a prood thing to hae yer banes put
awa' in Greyfriars, ance ye're through wi'
'em!"

"Nae doubt the gude auld man would rather
be alive on the Pentland braes than dead in
Greyfriars."

"Ay," the farmer admitted. "He was fair
fond o' the hills, an' no' likin' the toon. An',
mon, he was a wonder wi' the lambs. He'd gang
wi' a collie ower miles o' country in roarin'
weather, an' he'd aye fetch the lost sheep hame.
The auld mon was nane so weel furnished i' the
heid, but bairnies and beasts were unco' fond o'
'im. It wasna his fau't that Bobby was aye at
his heels. The lassie wad 'a' been after 'im, gin
'er mither had permeeted it."

Mr. Traill asked him why he had let so valuable
a man go, and the farmer replied at once that
he was getting old and could no longer do the
winter work. To any but a Scotchman brought
up near the sheep country this would have
sounded hard, but Mr. Traill knew that the farmers on the wild, tipped-up moors were themselves
hard pressed to meet rent and taxes. To keep
a shepherd incapacitated by age and liable to

lose a flock in a snow-storm, was to invite ruin.
And presently the man showed, unwittingly, how
sweet a kernel the heart may lie under the shell
of sordid necessity.

"I didna ken the auld man was fair ill or he
micht hae bided at the fairm an' tak'n 'is ain
time to dee at 'is ease."

As Bobby unrolled and stretched to an awak-
ening, the farmer got up, took him unaware and
thrust him into a covered basket. He had no
intention of letting the little creature give him
the slip again. Bobby howled at the indignity,
and struggled and tore at the stout wickerwork.
It went to Mr. Traill's heart to hear him, and to
see the gallant little dog so defenseless. He
talked to him through the latticed cover all the
way out to the cart, telling him Auld Jock meant
for him to go home. At that beloved name,
Bobby dropped to the bottom of the basket and
cried in such a heartbroken way that tears stood
in the landlord's eyes, and even the farmer confessed to a sudden "cauld in 'is heid."

"I'd gie 'im to ye, mon, gin it wasna that the
bit lassie wad greet her bonny een oot gin I didna
fetch 'im hame. Nae doot the bit tyke wad 'a'
deed gin ye hadna fed 'im."

"Eh, man, he'll no' bide with me, or I'd be
bargaining for him. And he'll no' be permitted

to live in the kirkyard. I know naething in this life more pitiful than a masterless, hameless dog." And then, to delay the moment of parting with Bobby, who stopped crying and began to lick his hand in frantic appeal through a hole in the basket, Mr. Traill asked how Bobby came by his name.

"It was a leddy o' the neeborhood o' Swanston. She cam' drivin' by Cauldbrae i' her bit cart wi' shaggy Shetlands to it an' stapped at the dairy for a drink o' buttermilk frae the kirn. Syne she saw the sonsie puppy loupin' at Auld Jock's heels, bonny as a poodle, but mair knowin'. The leddy gied me a poond note for 'im. I put 'im up on the seat, an' she said that noo she had a smart Hieland groom to match 'er Hieland steeds, an' she flicked the ponies wi' 'er whup. Syne the bit dog was on the airth an' flyin' awa' doon the road like the deil was after 'im. An' the leddy lauched an' lauched, an' went awa' wi'oot 'im. At the fut o' the brae she was still lauchin', an' she ca'ed back: 'Gie 'im the name o' Bobby, gude mon. He's left the plow-tail an's aff to Edinburgh to mak' his fame an' fortune.' I didna ken what the leddy meant."

"Man, she meant he was like Bobby Burns."

Here was a literary flavor that gave added attraction to a man who sat at the feet of the

Scottish muses. The landlord sighed as he went back to the doorway, and he stood there listening to the clatter of the cart and rough-shod horse and to the mournful howling of the little dog, until the sounds died away in Forest Road.

Mr. Traill would have been surprised to know, perhaps, that the confines of the city were scarcely passed before Bobby stopped protesting and grieving and settled down patiently to more profitable work. A human being thus kidnapped and carried away would have been quite helpless. But Bobby fitted his mop of a black muzzle into the largest hole of his wicker prison, and set his useful little nose to gathering news of his whereabouts.

If it should happen to a dog in this day to be taken from Ye Olde Greyfriars Dining-Rooms and carried southward out of Edinburgh there would be two miles or more of city and suburban streets to be traversed before coming to the open country. But a half century or more ago one could stand at the upper gate of Greyfriars kirk-yard or Heriot's Hospital grounds and look down a slope dotted with semi-rustic houses, a village or two and water-mills, and then cultivated farms, all the way to a stone-bridged burn and a toll-bar at the bottom of the valley. This hillside was the ancient Burghmuir where King James of old gathered a great host of Scots to march and fight and perish on Flodden Field.

Bobby had not gone this way homeward before, and was puzzled by the smell of prosperous little shops, and by the park-like odors from college campuses to the east, and from the well-kept residence park of George Square. But when the cart rattled across Lauriston Place he picked up the familiar scents of milk and wool from the cattle and sheep market, and then of cottage dooryards, of turned furrows and of farmsteads.

The earth wears ever a threefold garment of beauty. The human person usually manages to miss nearly everything but the appearance of things. A few of us are so fortunate as to have ears attuned to the harmonies woven on the wind by trees and birds and water; but the tricksy weft of odors that lies closest of all, enfolding the very bosom of the earth, escapes us. A little dog, traveling with his nose low, lives in another stratum of the world, and experiences other pleasures than his master. He has excitements that he does his best to share, and that send him flying in pursuit of phantom clues.

From the top of the Burghmuir it was easy going to Bobby. The snow had gone off in a thaw, releasing a multitude of autumnal aromas. There was a smell of birch and beech buds sealed up in gum, of berries clotted on the rowan-trees, and of balsam and spice from plantations of Highland firs and larches. The babbling water of the burn was scented with the dead bracken of glens down which it foamed. Even the leafless hedges had their woody odors, and stone dykes their musty smell of decaying mosses and lichens.

Bobby knew the pause at the toll-bar in the valley, and the mixed odors of many passing horses and men, there. He knew the smells of poultry and cheese at a dairy-farm; of hunting-dogs and riding-leathers at a sportsman's trysting inn, and of grist and polluted water at a mill. And after passing the hilltop toll-bar of Fairmilehead, dipping across a narrow valley and rounding the base of a sentinel peak, many tame odors were left behind. At the buildings of the large, scattered farms there were smells of sheep and dogs and barn-yards. But, for the most part, after the road began to climb over a high shoulder of the range, there was just one wild tang of heather and gorse and fern, tingling with salt air from the German Ocean.

When they reached Cauldbrae farm, high up on the slope, it was entirely dark. Lights in the small, deep-set windows gave the outlines of a low, steep-roofed, stone farm-house. Out of the darkness a little wind-blown figure of a lassie

fled down the brae to meet the cart, and an eager
little voice, as clear as a hill-bird's piping, cried
out:

"Hae ye got ma ain Bobby, faither?"

"Ay, lassie, I fetched 'im hame," the farmer
roared back, in his big voice.

Then the cart was stopped for the wee maid to
scramble up over a wheel, and there were sweet
little sounds of kissing and muffled little cud-
dlings under the warm plaid. When these soft
endearments had been attended to there was time
for another yearning.

"May I haud wee Bobby, faither?"

' 'Nae, lassie, a bonny bit bairnie couldna haud
'im in 'er sma' airms. Bobby's a' for gangin'
awa' to leev in a grand kirkyaird wi' Auld Jock."

A little gasp, and a wee sob, and an awed
question: "Is gude Auld Jock deid, daddy?"

Bobby heard it and answered with a mournful
howl. The lassie snuggled closer to the warm,
beating heart, hid her eyes in the rough plaid, and
cried for Auld Jock and for the grieving little dog.

"Niest to faither an' mither an' big brither
Wattie I lo'e Auld Jock an' Bobby." The
bairnie's voice was smothered in the plaidie.
Because it was dark and none were by to see,
the reticent Scot could overflow in tender speech.
His arm tightened around this one little ewe

lamb of the human fold on cold slope farm. He comforted the child by telling her how they would mak' it up to Bobby, and how very soon a wee dog forgets the keenest sorrow and is happy again.

The sheep-dogs charged the cart with as deafening a clamor of welcome as if a home-coming had never happened before, and raced the horse across the level. The kitchen door flared open, a sudden beacon to shepherds scattered afar on these upland billows of heath. In a moment the basket was in the house, the door snecked, and Bobby released on the hearth.

It was a beautiful, dark old kitchen, with a homely fire of peat that glowed up to smoke-stained rafters. Soon it was full of shepherds, come in to a supper of brose, cheese, milk and bannocks. Sheep-dogs sprawled and dozed on the hearth, so that the gude wife complained of their being underfoot. But she left them undisturbed and stepped over them, for, tired as they were, they would have to go out again to drive the sheep into the fold.

Humiliated by being brought home a prisoner, and grieving for the forsaken grave in Greyfriars, Bobby crept away to a corner bench, on which Auld Jock had always sat in humble self-efface-ment. He lay down under it, and the little four year-old lassie sat on the floor close beside him, understanding, and sorry with him. Her rough brother Wattie teased her about wanting her supper there on one plate with Bobby.

"I wadna gang daft aboot a bit dog, Elsie."

"Leave the bairn by 'er lane," commanded the farmer. The mither patted the child's bright head, and wiped the tears from the bluebell eyes. And there was a little sobbing confidence poured into a sympathetic ear.

Bobby refused to eat at first, but by and by he thought better of it. A little dog that has his life to live and his work to do must have fuel to drive the throbbing engine of his tiny heart. So Bobby very sensibly ate a good supper in the lassie's company and, grateful for that and for her sympathy, submitted to her shy petting. But after the shepherds and dogs were gone and the farmer had come in again from an overseeing look about the place the little dog got up, trotted to the door, and lay down by it. The lassie followed him. With two small, plump hands she pushed Bobby's silver veil back, held his muzzle and looked into his sad, brown eyes.

"Oh, mither, mither, Bobby's greetin'," she cried.

"Nae, bonny wee, a sma' dog canna greet."

"Ay, he's greetin' sair!"

A sudden, sweet little sound was dropped on Bobby's head.

"Ye shouldna kiss the bit dog, bairnie. He isna like a human body."

"Ay, a wee kiss is gude for 'im. Faither, he greets so I canna thole it." The child fled to comforting arms in the inglenook and cried herself to sleep. The gude wife knitted, and the gude mon smoked by the pleasant fire. The only sound in the room was the ticking of the wag-at-the-wa' clock, for burning peat makes no noise at all, only a pungent whiff in the nostrils, the memory of which gives a Scotch laddie abroad a fit of hamesickness. Bobby lay very still and watchful by the door. The farmer served his astonishing news in dramatic bits.

"Auld Jock's deid." Bobby stirred at that, and flattened out on the floor.

"Ay, the lassie told that, an' I wad hae kenned it by the dog. He is greetin' by the ordinar'."

"An' he's buried i' the kirkyaird o' auld Greyfriars." Ah, that fetched her! The gude wife dropped her knitting and stared at him.

"There's a gairdener, like at the country-hooses o' the gentry, leevin' in a bit lodge by the gate. He has naethin' to do, ava, but lock the gate at nicht, put the dogs oot, an' mak' the posies bloom i' the simmer. Ay, it's a bonny place."

"It's ower grand for Auld Jock."

"Ye may weel say that. His bit grave isna so far frae the martyrs' monument." When the grandeur of that had sunk in he went on to other incredibilities.

Presently he began to chuckle. "There's a bit notice on the gate that nae dogs are admittet, but Bobby's sleepit on Auld Jock's grave ane —twa—three—fower nichts, an' the gairdener doesna ken it, ava. He's a canny beastie."

"Ay, he is. Folk wull be comin' frae miles aroond juist to leuk at the sperity bit. Ilka body aboot kens Auld Jock. It' ll be maist michty news to tell at the kirk on the Sabbath, that he's buried i' Greyfriars."

Through all this talk Bobby had lain quietly by the door, in the expectation that it would be unlatched. Impatient of delay, he began to whimper and to scratch on the panel. The lassie opened her blue eyes at that, scrambled down, and ran to him. Instantly Bobby was up, tugging at her short little gown and begging to be let out. When she clasped her chubby arms around his neck and tried to comfort him he struggled free and set up a dreadful howling.

"Hoots, Bobby, stap yer havers!" shouted the farmer.

"Eh, lassie, he'll deave us a'. We'll juist hae

to put 'im i' the byre wi' the coos for the nicht," cried the distracted mither.

"I want Bobby i' the bed wi' me. I'll cuddle 'im an' lo'e 'im till he staps greetin'."

"Nae, bonny wee, he wullna stap." The farmer picked the child up on one arm, gripped the dog under the other, and the gude wife went before with a lantern, across the dark farm-yard to the cow-barn. When the stout door was unlatched there was a smell of warm animals, of milk, and cured hay, and the sound of full, contented breathings that should have brought a sense of companionship to a grieving little creature.

"Bobby wullna be lanely here wi' the coos, bairnie, an' i' the morn ye can tak' a bit rope an' haud it in a wee hand so he canna brak awa', an' syne, in a day or twa, he'll be forgettin' Auld Jock. Ay, ye'll hae grand times wi' the sonsie doggie, rinnin' an' loupin' on the braes."

This argument was so convincing and so attractive that the little maid dried her tears, kissed Bobby on the head again, and made a bed of heather for him in a corner. But as they were leaving the byre fresh doubts assailed her.

"He'll gang awa' gin ye dinna tie 'im snug the nicht, faither."

"Sic a fulish bairn! Wi' fower wa's aroond

GREYFRIARS BCBBY

'im, an' a roof to 'is heid, an' a floor to 'is fut,
hoo could a sma' dog mak' a way oot?''

It was a foolish notion, bred of fond anxiety, and
so, reassured, the child went happily back to the
house and t⟩ rosy sleep in her little closet bed.

Ah! here was a warm place in a cold world for
Bobby. A soft-hearted little mistress and merry
playmate was here, generous food, and human
society of a kind that was very much to a little
farm dog's liking. Here was freedom — wide
moors to delight his scampering legs, adventures
with rabbits, foxes, hares and moor - fowl, and
great spaces where no one's ears would be offended by his loudest, longest barking. Besides,
Auld Jock had said, with his last breath, "Gang
—awa'—hame—laddie!" It is not to be supposed Bobby had forgotten that, since he remembered and obeyed every other order of that
beloved voice. But there, self-interest, love of
liberty, and the instinct of obedience, even, sank
into the abysses of the little creature's mind. Up
to the top rose the overmastering necessity of
guarding the bit of sacred earth that covered
his master.

The byre was no sooner locked than Bobby
began, in the pitch darkness, to explore the walls.
The single promise of escape that was offered
was an inch-wide crack under the door, where

the flooring stopped short and exposed a strip
of earth. That would have appalled any but
a desperate little dog. The crack was so small
as to admit but one paw, at first, and the earth
was packed as hard as wood by generations of
trampling cattle.

There he began to dig. He came of a breed of
dogs used by farmers and hunters to dig small,
burrowing animals out of holes, a breed whose
courage and persistence know no limit. He dug
patiently, steadily, hour after hour, enlarging the
hole by inches. Now and then he had to stop to
rest. When he was able to use both forepaws
he made encouraging progress; but when he had
to reach under the door, quite the length of his
stretched legs, and drag every bit of earth back
into the byre, the task must have been impossible to any little creature not urged by utter
misery. But Skye terriers have been known to
labor with such fury that they have perished of
their own exertions. Bobby's nose sniffed liberty
long before he could squeeze his weasel-like body
through the tunnel. His back bruised and
strained by the struggle through a hole too
small, he stood, trembling with exhaustion, in the
windy dawn.

An opening door, a barking sheep-dog, the
shuffle of the moving flock, were signs that the

farm day was beginning, although all the stars had not faded out of the sky. A little flying shadow, Bobby slipped out of the cow-yard, past the farm-house, and literally tumbled down the brae. From one level to another he dropped, several hundred feet in a very few minutes, and from the clear air of the breezy hill-top to a nether world that was buried fathoms deep in a sea-fog as white as milk.

Hidden in a deep fold of the spreading skirts of the range, and some distance from the road, lay a pool, made by damming a burn, and used, in the shearing season, for washing sheep. Surrounded by brushy woods, and very damp and dark, at other seasons it was deserted. Bobby found this secluded place with his nose, curled up under a hazel thicket and fell sound asleep. And while he slept, a nipping wind from the far, northern Highlands swooped down on the mist and sent it flying out to sea. The Lowlands cleared like magic. From the high point where Bobby lay the road could be seen to fall, by short rises and long descents, all the way to Edinburgh. From its crested ridge and flanking hills the city trailed a dusky banner of smoke out over the fishing fleet in the Firth.

A little dog cannot see such distant views. Bobby could only read and follow the guideposts of odors along the way. He had begun the ascent to the toll-bar when he heard the clatter of a cart and the pounding of hoofs behind him. He did not wait to learn if this was the Cauldbrae farmer in pursuit. Certain knowledge on that point was only to be gained at his peril. He sprang into the shelter of a stone wall, scrambled over it, worked his way along it a short distance, and disappeared into a brambly path that skirted a burn in a woody dell.

Immediately the little dog was lost in an un-explored country. The narrow glen was musical with springs, and the low growth was undercut with a maze of rabbit runs, very distracting to a dog of a hunting breed. Bobby knew, by much journeying with Auld Jock, that running water is a natural highway. Sheep drift along the low-est level until they find an outlet down some declivity, or up some foaming steep, to new pastures.

But never before had Bobby found, above such a rustic brook, a many chimneyed and gabled house of stone, set in a walled garden and swathed in trees. To-day, many would cross wide seas to look upon Swanston cottage, in whose odorous old garden a whey-faced, wistful-eyed laddie dreamed so many brave and laughing dreams. It was only a farm-house then, fallen from a more romantic history, and it had no attraction for Bobby. He merely sniffed at dead vines of clematis, sleeping briar bushes, and very live, bright hedges of holly, rounded a corner of its wall, and ran into a group of lusty children romping on the brae, below the very prettiest, thatch-roofed and hill-sheltered hamlet within many a mile of Edinboro' town. The bairns were lunching from grimy, mittened hands, gypsy fashion, life being far too short and playtime too brief for formal meals. Seeing them eating, Bobby suddenly discovered that he was hungry. He rose before a well-provided laddie and politely begged for a share of his meal.

Such an excited shouting of admiration and calling on mithers to come and see the bonny wee dog was never before heard on Swanston village green. Doors flew open and bareheaded women ran out. Then the babies had to be brought, and the old grandfaithers and grandmithers. Everybody oh-ed and ah-ed and clapped hands, and doubled up with laughter, for, a tempting bit held playfully just out of reach, Bobby rose, again and again, jumped for it, and chased a teasing laddie. Then he bethought him to roll over and over, and to go through other winsome little tricks, as Auld Jock had taught him to do, to win the reward. All this had one quite unexpected result. A shrewd-eyed woman pounced upon Bobby and captured him.

"He's no' an ordinar' dog. Some leddy has lost her pet. I'll juist shut 'im up, an' syne she'll pay a shullin' or twa to get 'im again."

With a twist and a leap Bobby was gone. He scrambled straight up the steep, thorn-clad wall of the glen, where no laddie could follow, and was over the crest. It was a narrow escape, made by terrific effort. His little heart pounding with exhaustion and alarm, he hid under a whin bush to get his breath and strength. The sheltered dell was windless, but here a stiff breeze blew. Suddenly shifting a point, the wind brought to the little dog's nose a whiff of the acrid coal smoke of Edinburgh three miles away.

Straight as an arrow he ran across country, over roadway and wall, plowed fields and rippling burns. He scrambled under hedges and dashed across farmsteads and cottage gardens. As he neared the city the hour bells aided him, for the Skye terrier is keen of hearing. It was growing dark when he climbed up the last bank and gained Lauriston Place. There he picked up the odors of milk and wool, and the damp smell of the kirkyard.

Now for something comforting to put into his famished little body. A night and a day of exhausting work, of anxiety and grief, had used up the last ounce of fuel. Bobby raced down Forest Road and turned the slight angle into Greyfriars Place. The lamp-lighter's progress toward the bridge was marked by the double row of lamps that bloomed, one after one, on the dusk. The little dog had come to the steps of Mr. Traill's place, and lifted himself to scratch on the door, when the bugle began to blow. He dropped with the first note and dashed to the kirkyard gate.

None too soon! Mr. Brown was setting the little wicket gate inside, against the wall. In the instant his back was turned, Bobby slipped through. After nightfall, when the caretaker had made his rounds, he came out from under the fallen table-tomb of Mistress Jean Grant.

Lights appeared at the rear windows of the tenements, and families sat at supper. It was snell weather again, the sky dark with threat of snow, and the windows were all closed. But with a sharp bark beneath the lowest of them Bobby could have made his presence and his wants known. He watched the people eating, sitting wistfully about on his haunches here and there, but remaining silent. By and by there were sounds of crying babies, of crockery being washed, and the ringing of church bells far and near. Then the lights were extinguished, and huge bulks of shadow, of tenements and kirk, engulfed the kirkyard.

When Bobby lay down on Auld Jock's grave, pellets of frozen snow were falling and the air had hardened toward frost.

VI

SLEEP alone goes far to revive a little dog, and fasting sharpens the wits. Bobby was so tired that he slept soundly, but so hungry that he woke early, and instantly alert to his situation. It was so very early of a dark winter morning that not even the sparrows were out foraging in the kirkyard for dry seeds. The drum and bugle had not been sounded from the Castle when the milk and dustman's carts began to clatter over the frozen streets. With the first hint of dawn stout fishwives, who had tramped all the way in from the piers of Newhaven with heavily laden creels on their heads, were lustily crying their "caller herrin'." Soon fagot men began to call up the courts of tenements, where fuel was bought by the scant bundle: "Are ye cauld?"

Many a human waif in the tall buildings about the lower end of Greyfriars kirkyard was cold, even in bed, but, in his thick underjacket of fleece, Bobby was as warm as a plate of breakfast toast. With a vigorous shaking he broke and scattered the crust of snow that burdened his shaggy thatch. Then he lay down on the grave

again, with his nose on his paws. Urgent matters occupied the little dog's mind. To deal with
these affairs he had the long head of the canniest
Scot, wide and high between the ears, and a
muzzle as determined as a little steel trap. Small
and forlorn as he was, courage, resource and
purpose marked him.

As soon as the door of the caretaker's lodge
opened he would have to creep under the fallen
slab again. To lie in such a cramped position,
hour after hour, day after day, was enough to
break the spirit of any warm-blooded creature
that lives. It was an exquisite form of torture
not long to be endured. And to get his single
meal a day at Mr. Traill's place Bobby had to
watch for the chance opening of the wicket to
slip in and out like a thief. The furtive life is
not only perilous, it outrages every feeling of an
honest dog. It is hard for him to live at all without the approval and the cordial consent of men.
The human order hostile, he quickly loses his
self-respect and drops to the Pariah class.
Already wee Bobby had the look of the neglected. His pretty coat was dirty and unkempt.
In his run across country, leaves, twigs and burrs
had become entangled in his long hair, and his
legs and underparts were caked with mire.

Instinctively any dog struggles to escape the

fate of the outcast. By every art he possesses he ingratiates himself with men. One that has his usefulness in the human scheme of things often is able to make his own terms with life, to win the niche of his choice. Bobby's one talent that was of practical value to society was his hunting instinct for every small animal that burrows and prowls and takes toll of men's labor. In Greyfriars kirkyard was work to be done that he could do. For quite three centuries rats and mice had multiplied in this old sanctuary garden from which cats were chased and dogs excluded. Every breeze that blew carried challenges to Bobby's offended nose. Now, in the crisp gray dawn, a big rat came out into the open and darted here and there over the powdering of dry snow that frosted the kirkyard.

A leap, as if released from a spring, and Bobby captured it. A snap of his long muzzle, a jerk of his stoutly set head, and the victim hung limp from his grip. And he followed another deeply seated instinct when he carried the slain to Auld Jock's grave. Trophies of the chase were always to be laid at the feet of the master.

"Gude dog! eh, but ye're a bonny wee fechter!" Auld Jock had always said after such an exploit; and Bobby had been petted and praised until he nearly wagged his crested tail off with happiness

and pride. Then he had been given some choice
tidbit of food as a reward for his prowess. The
farmer of Cauldbrae had on such occasions admitted that Bobby might be of use about barn
and dairy, and Mr. Traill had commended his
capture of prowlers in the dining-room. But
Bobby was "ower young" and had not been
"put to the vermin" as a definite business in life.
He caught a rat, now and then, as he chased
rabbits, merely as a diversion. When he had
caught this one he lay down again. But after a
time he got up deliberately and trotted down to
the encircling line of old courtyarded tombs.
There were nooks and crannies between and behind these along the wall into which the caretaker could not penetrate with sickle, rake and
spade, that formed sheltered runways for rodents.

A long, low, weasel-like dog that could flatten
himself on the ground, Bobby squeezed between
railings and pedestals, scrambled over fallen
fragments of sculptured urns, trumpets, angels'
wings, altars, skull and cross-bones, and Latin-
inscribed scrolls. He went on his stomach under
holly and laurel shrubs, burdocks, thistles, and
tangled, dead vines. Here and there he lay in
such rubbish as motionless as the effigies carven
on marble biers. With the growing light grew
the heap of the slain on Auld Jock's grave.

GREYFRIARS BOBBY

Having done his best, Bobby lay down again, worse in appearance than before, but with a stouter heart. He did not stir, although the shadows fled, the sepulchers stood up around the field of snow, and slabs and shafts camped in ranks on the slope. Smoke began to curl up from high, clustered chimney-pots; shutters were opened, and scantily clad women had hurried errands on decaying gallery and reeling stairway. Suddenly the Castle turrets were gilded with pale sunshine, and all the little cells in the tall, old houses hummed and buzzed and clacked with life. The University bell called scattered students to morning prayers. Pinched and elfish faces of children appeared at the windows overlooking the kirkyard. The sparrows had instant news of that, and the little winged beggars fluttered up to the lintels of certain deep-set casements, where ill-fed bairns scattered breakfasts of crumbs.

Bobby watched all this without a movement. He shivered when the lodge door was heard to open and shut and heavy footsteps crunched on the gravel and snow around the church. "Juist fair silly" on his quaking legs he stood up, head and tail drooped. But he held his ground bravely, and when the caretaker sighted him he trotted to meet the man, lifted himself on his hind legs, his short, shagged fore paws on his breast, begging attention and indulgence. Then he sprawled across the great boots, asking pardon for the liberty he was taking. At last, all in a flash, he darted back to the grave, sniffed at it, and stood again, head up, plumy tail crested, all excitement, as much as to say:

"Come awa' ower, man, an' leuk at the braw sicht."

If he could have barked, his meaning would have carried more convincingly, but he "hauded 'is gab" loyally. And, alas, the caretaker was not to be beguiled. Mr. Traill had told him Bobby had been sent back to the hill farm, but here he was, "perseestent" little rascal, and making some sort of bid for the man's favor. Mr. Brown took his pipe out of his mouth in surprised exasperation, and glowered at the dog.

"Gang awa' oot wi' ye!"

But Bobby was back again coaxing undauntedly, abasing himself before the angry man, in sisting that he had something of interest to show. The caretaker was literally badgered and cajoled into following him. One glance at the formidable heap of the slain, and Mr. Brown dropped to a seat on the slab.

"Preserve us a'!"

He stared from the little dog to his victims

turned them over with his stout stick and counted them, and stared again. Bobby fixed his pleading eyes on the man and stood at strained attention while fate hung in the balance.

"Gude wark! Gude wark! A braw doggie, an' an unco' fechter. Losh! but ye're a deil o' a bit dog!"

All this was said in a tone of astonished comment, so non-committal of feeling that Bobby's tail began to twitch in the stress of his anxiety. When the caretaker spoke again, after a long, puzzled frowning, it was to express a very human bewilderment and irritation.

"Noo, what am I gangin' to do wi' ye?"

Ah, that was encouraging! A moment before, he had ordered Bobby out in no uncertain tone. After another moment he referred the question to a higher court.

" Jeanie, woman, come awa' oot a meenit, wull ye?"

A hasty pattering of carpet-slippered feet on the creaking snow, around the kirk, and there was the neatest little apple-cheeked peasant woman in Scotland, "snod" from her smooth, frosted hair, spotless linen mutch and lawn kerchief, to her white, lamb's-wool stockings.

"Here's the bit dog I was tellin' ye aboot; an' see for yersel' what he's done noo."

"The wee beastie couldna do a' that! It's as muckle as his ain wecht in fou' vermin!" she cried.

"Ay, he did. Thae terriers are sperity, by the ordinar'. Ane o' them, let into the corn exchange a murky nicht, killed saxty in ten meenits, an' had to be dragged awa' by the tail. Noo, what I am gangin' to do wi' the takin' bit I dinna ken."

It is very certain that simple Mistress Jean Brown had never heard of Mr. Dick's advice to Miss Betsy Trotwood on the occasion when young David Copperfield presented himself, travel-stained and weary, before his good aunt. But out of her experience of wholesome living she brought forth the same wise opinion.

"I'd gie him a gude washin' first of a', Jamie. He leuks like some puir, gaen-aboot dog." And she drew her short, blue-stuff gown back from Bobby's grateful attentions.

Mr. Brown slapped his corduroy-breeked knee and nodded his grizzled head. "Richt ye are. It's maist michty, noo, I wadna think o' that. When I was leevin' as an under gairdener wi' a laird i' Argyleshire I was aye aboot the kennels wi' the gillies. That was lang syne. The sma' terrier dogs were aye washed i' claes tubs wi' warm water an' soap. Come awa', Bobby."

GREYFRIARS BOBBY

The caretaker got up stiffly, for such snell weather was apt to give him twinges in his joints. In him a youthful enthusiasm for dogs had suddenly revived. Besides, although he would have denied it, he was relieved at having the main issue, as to what was to be done with this four-footed trespasser, side-tracked for a time. Bobby followed him to the lodge at an eager trot, and he dutifully hopped into the bath that was set on the rear doorstep. Mr. Brown scrubbed him vigorously, and Bobby splashed and swam and churned the soapy water to foam. He scrambled out at once, when told to do so, and submitted to being dried with a big, tow-linen towel. This was all a delightful novelty to Bobby. Heretofore he had gone into any convenient tarn or burn to swim, and then dried himself by rolling on the heather and running before the wind. Now he was bundled up ignominiously in an old flannel petticoat, carried across a sanded kitchen floor and laid on a warm hearth.

"Doon wi' ye!" was the gruff order. Bobby turned around and around on the hearth, like some little wild dog making a bed in the jungle, before he obeyed. He kept very still during the reading of a chapter and the singing of a Psalm, as he had been taught to do at the farm by many a reminder from Auld Jock's boot. And he kept away from the breakfast - table, although the walls of his stomach were collapsed as flat as the sides of an empty pocket.

It was such a clean, shining little kitchen, with the scoured deal table, chairs and cupboard, and the firelight from the grate winked so on pewter mugs, copper kettle, willow-patterned plates and diamond panes, that Bobby blinked too. Flowers bloomed in pots on the casement sills, and a little brown skylark sang, fluttering as if it would soar, in a gilded cage. After the morning meal Mr. Brown lighted his pipe and put on his bonnet to go out again, when he bethought him that Bobby might be needing something to eat.

"What 'll ye gie 'im, Jeanie? At the laird's, noo, the terriers were aye fed wi' bits o' livers an' cheese an' moor-fowls' eggs, an' sic-like, fried."

"Havers, Jamie, it's no' releegious to feed a dog better than puir bairns. He'll do fair weel wi' table scraps."

She set down a plate with a spoonful of porridge on it, a cold potato, some bread crusts, and the leavings of a broiled caller herrin'. It was a generous breakfast for so small a dog, but Bobby had been without food for quite forty hours, and had done an amazing amount of work in the meantime. When he had eaten all of it he was still hungry. As a polite hint, he polished the empty plate with his pink tongue and looked up expectantly; but the best-intentioned people, if they have had little to do with dogs, cannot read such signs.

"Ye needna lick the posies aff," the wifie said, good-humoredly, as she picked the plate up to wash it. She thought to put down a tin basin of water. Bobby lapped it so eagerly, yet so daintily, that she added: "He's a weel-broucht-up tyke, Jamie."

"He is so. Noo, we'll see hoo weel he can leuk." In a shamefaced way he fetched from a tool-box a long-forgotten, strong little curry-comb, such as is used on shaggy Shetland ponies. With that he proceeded to give Bobby such a grooming as he had never had before. It was a painful operation, for his thatch was a stubborn mat of crisp waves and knotty tangles to his plumy tail and down to his feathered toes. He braced himself and took the punishment without a whimper, and when it was done he stood cascaded with dark-silver ripples nearly to the floor.

"The bonny wee!" cried Mistress Jeanie. "I canna tak' ma twa een aff o' 'im."

"Ay, he's bonny by the ordinar'. It wad be

grand, noo, gin the meenister'd fancy 'im an tak' 'im into the manse."

The wifie considered this ruefully. "Jamie,] was wishin' ye didna hae to—"

But what she wished he did not have to do, Mr. Brown did not stop to hear. He suddenly clapped his bonnet on his head and went out. He had an urgent errand on High Street, to buy grass and flower seeds and tools that would certainly be needed in April. It took him an hour or more of shrewd looking about for the best bargains, in a swarm of little barnacle and cellar shops, to spend a few of the kirk's shillings. When he found himself, to his disgust, looking at a nail-studded collar for a little dog he called himself a "doited auld fule," and tramped back across the bridge.

At the kirkyard gate he stopped and read the notice through twice: "No dogs permitted." That was as plain as "Thou shalt not." To the pious caretaker and trained servant it was the eleventh commandment. He shook his head, sighed, and went in to dinner. Bobby was not in the house, and the master of it avoided inquiring for him. He also avoided the wifie's wistful eye, and he busied himself inside the two kirks all the afternoon.

Because he was in the kirks, and the beautiful

memorial windows of stained glass were not for the purpose of looking out, he did not see a dramatic incident that occurred in the kirkyard after three o'clock in the afternoon. The prelude to it really began with the report of the time-gun at one. Bobby had insisted upon being let out of the lodge kitchen, and had spent the morning near Auld Jock's grave and in nosing about neighboring slabs and thorn bushes. When the time-gun boomed he trotted to the gate quite openly and waited there inside the wicket.

In such nipping weather there were no visitors to the kirkyard and the gate was not opened. The music bells ran the gamut of old Scotch airs and ceased, while he sat there and waited patiently. Once a man stopped to look at the little dog, and Bobby promptly jumped on the wicket, plainly begging to have it unlatched. But the passer-by decided that some lady had left her pet behind, and would return for him. So he patted the attractive little Highlander on the head and went on about his business.

Discouraged by the unpromising outlook for dinner that day, Bobby went slowly back to the grave. Twice afterward he made hopeful pilgrimages to the gate. For diversion he fell noiselessly upon a prowling cat and chased it out

of the kirkyard. At last he sat upon the table
tomb. He had escaped notice from the tenements all the morning because the view from
most of the windows was blocked by washings,
hung out and dripping, then freezing and clapping
against the old tombs. It was half-past three
o'clock when a tiny, wizened face popped out of
one of the rude little windows in the decayed
Cunzie Neuk at the bottom of Candlemakers
Row. Crippled Tammy Barr called out in shrill
excitement:

"Ailie! O-o-oh, Ailie Lindsey, there's the wee
doggie!"

"Whaur?" The lassie's elfin face looked out
from a low, rear window of the Candlemakers'
Guildhall at the top of the Row.

"On the stane by the kirk wa'."

"I see 'im noo. Isna he bonny? I wish
Bobby could bide i' the kirkyaird, but they
wadna let 'im. Tammy, gin ye tak' 'im up to
Maister Traill, he'll gie ye the shullin'!"

"I couldna tak' 'im by ma lane," was the
pathetic confession. "Wad ye gang wi' me,
Ailie? Ye could drap ower an' catch 'im, an' I
could come by the gate. Faither made me some
grand crutches frae an' auld chair back."

Tears suddenly drowned the lassie's blue eyes
and ran down her pinched little cheeks. "Nae

I couldna gang. I haena ony shoon to ma feet."

"It's no' so cauld. Gin I had twa gude feet I could gang the bit way wi'oot shoon."

"I ken it isna so cauld," Ailie admitted, "but for a lassie it's no' respectable to gang to a grand place barefeeted."

That was undeniable, and the eager children fell silent and tearful. But oh, necessity is the mother of makeshifts among the poor! Suddenly Ailie cried: "Bide a meenit, Tammy," and vanished. Presently she was back, with the difficulty overcome. "Grannie says I can wear her shoon. She doesna wear 'em i' the hoose, ava."

"I'll gie ye a saxpence, Ailie," offered Tammy.

The sordid bargain shocked no feeling of these tenement bairns nor marred their pleasure in the adventure. Presently there was a tap-tap-tapping of crutches on the heavy gallery that fronted the Cunzie Neuk, and on the stairs that descended from it to the steep and curving Row. The lassie draped a fragment of an old plaid deftly over her thinly clad shoulders, climbed through the window, to the pediment of the classic tomb that blocked it, and dropped into the kirkyard. To her surprise Bobby was there at her feet, frantically wagging his tail, and he raced her to the gate. She caught him on the steps of the dining-room, and held his wriggling little body, fast until Tammy came up.

It was a tumultuous little group that burst in upon the astonished landlord: barking fluff of an excited dog, flying lassie in clattering big shoes, and wee, tapping Tammy. They literally fell upon him when he was engaged in counting out his money.

"Whaur did you find him?" asked Mr Traill in bewilderment.

Six-year-old Ailie slipped a shy finger into her mouth, and looked to the very much more mature five-year-old crippled laddie to answer:

"He was i' the kirkyaird."

"Sittin' upon a stane by 'is ainsel'," added Ailie.

"An' no' hidin', ava. It was juist like he was leevin' there."

"An' syne, when I drapped oot o' the window he louped at me so bonny, an' I couldna keep up wi' 'im to the gate."

Wonder of wonders! It was plain that Bobby had made his way back from the hill farm and, from his appearance and manner, as well as from this account, it was equally clear that some happy change in his fortunes had taken place. He sat up on his haunches listening with interest

and lolling his tongue! And that was a thing
the bereft little dog had rot done since his master died. In the first pause in the talk he rose
and begged for his dinner.

"Noo, what am I to pay? It took ane, twa,
three o' ye to fetch ane sma' dog. A saxpence
for the laddie, a saxpence for the lassie, an' a bit
meal for Bobby."

While he was putting the plate down under
the settle Mr. Traill heard an amazed whisper:
"He's gien the doggie a chuckie bane." The
landlord switched the plate from under Bobby's
protesting little muzzle and turned to catch the
hungry look on the faces of the children Chicken,
indeed, for a little dog, before these ill-fed bairns!
Mr. Traill had a brilliant thought.

"Preserve me! I didna think to eat ma ain
dinner. I hae so muckle to eat I canna eat it by
ma lane."

The idea of having too much to eat was so
preposterously funny that Tammy doubled up
with laughter and nearly tumbled over his
crutches. Mr. Traill set him upright again.

"Did ye ever gang on a picnic, bairnies?"
And what was a picnic? Tammy ventured the
opinion that it might be some kind of a cart for
lame laddies to ride in.

"A picnic is when ye gang gypsying in the

summer," Mr. Traill explained. "Ye walk to a bonny green brae, an' sit doon under a hawthorn-tree a' covered wi' posies, by a babblin' burn, an' ye eat oot o' yer ain hands. An' syne ye hear a throstle or a redbreast sing an' a saucy black-bird whustle."

"Could ye tak' a dog?" asked Tammy.

"Ye could that, mannie. It's no' a picnic wi'oot a sonsie doggie to rin on the brae wi' ye."

"Oh!" Ailie's blue eyes slowly widened in her pallid little face. "But ye couldna hae a picnic i' the snawy weather."

"Ay, ye could. It's the bonniest of a' when ye're no' expectin' it. I aye keep a picnic hidden i' the ingleneuk aboon." He suddenly swung Tammy up on his shoulder, and calling, gaily, "Come awa'," went out the door, through another beside it, and up a flight of stairs to the dining-room above. A fire burned there in the grate, the tables were covered with linen, and there were blooming flowers in pots in the front windows. Patrons from the University, and the well-to-do streets and squares to the south and east, made of this upper room a sort of club in the evenings. At four o'clock in the afternoon there were no guests.

"Noo," said Mr. Traill, when his overcome

little guests were seated at a table in the ingle
nook. "A picnic is whaur ye hae onything ye
fancy to eat; gude things ye wullna be haein'
ilka day, ye mind." He rang a call-bell, and a
grinning waiter laddie popped up so quickly the
lassie caught her breath.

"Eneugh broo for aince," said Tammy.

"Porridge that isna burned," suggested Ailie.
Such pitiful poverty of the imagination!

"Nae, it's bread, an' butter, an' strawberry
jam, an' tea wi' cream an' sugar, an' cauld
chuckie at a snawy picnic," announced Mr.
Traill. And there it was, served very quickly
and silently, after some manner of magic. Bobby
had to stand on the fourth chair to eat his
dinner, and when he had despatched it he sat up
and viewed the little party with the liveliest
interest and happiness.

"Tammy," Ailie said, when her shyness had
worn off, "it's like the grand tales ye mak' up i'
yer heid."

"Preserve me! Does the wee mannie mak' up
stories?"

"It's juist fulish things, aboot haein' mair to
eat, an' a sonsie doggie to play wi', an' twa gude
legs to tak' me aboot. I think 'em oot at nicht
when I canna sleep."

"Eh, laddie, do ye noo?" Mr. Traill suddenly

had a terrible "cauld in 'is heid," that made his eyes water. "Hoo auld are ye?"

"Five, gangin' on sax."

"Losh! I thoucht ye war fifty, gangin' on saxty." Laughter saved the day from over-moist emotions. And presently Mr. Traill was able to say in a business-like tone:

"We'll hae to tak' ye to the infirmary. An' if they canna mak' yer legs ower ye'll get a pair o' braw crutches that are the niest thing to gude legs. An' syne we'll see if there's no' a place in Heriot's for a sma' laddie that mak's up bonny tales o' his ain in the murky auld Cunzie Neuk."

Now the gay little feast was eaten, and early dark was coming on. If Mr. Traill had entertained the hope that Bobby had recovered from his grief and might remain with him he was disappointed. The little dog began to be restless. He ran to the door and back; he begged, and he scratched on the panel. And then he yelped! As soon as the door was opened he shot out of it, tumbled down the stairway and waited at the foot impatiently for the lower door to be unlatched. Ailie's thin, swift legs were left behind when Bobby dashed to the kirkyard.

Tammy followed at a surprising pace on his rude crutches, and Mr. Traill brought up the rear. If the children could not smuggle the frantic little dog inside the landlord meant to put him over the wicket and, if necessary, to have it out with the caretaker, and then to go before the kirk minister and officers with his plea. He was still concealed by the buildings, from the alcoved gate, when he heard Mr. Brown's gruff voice taking the frightened bairns to task.

"Gie me the dog; an' dinna ye tak' him oot ony mair wi'oot spierin' me."

The children fled. Peeping around the angle of the Book Hunter's Stall, Mr. Traill saw the caretaker lift Bobby over the wicket to his arms, and start with him toward the lodge. He was perishing with curiosity about this astonishing change of front on the part of Mr. Brown, but it was a delicate situation in which it seemed best not to meddle. He went slowly back to the restaurant, begrudging Bobby to the luckier caretaker.

His envy was premature. Mr. Brown set Bobby inside the lodge kitchen and announced briefly to his wife: "The bit dog wull sleep i' the hoose the nicht." And he went about some business at the upper end of the kirkyard. When he came in an hour later Bobby was gone.

"I couldna keep 'im in, Jamie. He didna blatter, but he greeted so sair to be let oot, an syne he scratched a' the paint aff the door."

Mr. Brown glowered at her in exasperation. "Woman, they'll hae me up afore kirk sessions for brakin' the rules, an' syne they'll turn us a' oot i' the cauld warld togither."

He slammed the door and stormed angrily around the kirk. It was still light enough to see the little creature on the snowy mound and, indeed, Bobby got up and wagged his tail in friendly greeting. At that all the bluster went out of the man, and he began to argue the matter with the dog.

"Come awa', Bobby. Ye canna be leevin' i' the kirkyaird."

Bobby was of a different opinion. He turned around and around, thoughtfully, several times, then sat up on the grave. Entirely willing to spend a social hour with his new friend, he fixed his eyes hospitably upon him. Mr. Brown dropped to the slab, lighted his pipe, and smoked for a time, to compose his agitated mind. By and by he got up briskly and stooped to lift the little dog. At that Bobby dug his claws in the clods and resisted with all his muscular body and determined mind. He clung to the grave so desperately, and looked up so piteously, that the caretaker surrendered. And there was snod Mistress Jeanie, forgetting her spotless gown and kneeling in the snow.

GREYFRIARS BOBBY

"Puir Bobby, puir wee Bobby!' she cried, and her tears fell on the little tousled head. The caretaker strode abruptly away and waited for the wifie in the shadow of the auld kirk. Bobby lifted his muzzle and licked the caressing hand. Then he curled himself up comfortably on the mound and went to sleep.

VII

IN no part of Edinburgh did summer come up earlier, or with more lavish bloom, than in old Greyfriars kirkyard. Sheltered on the north and east, it was open to the moist breezes of the southwest, and during all the lengthening afternoons the sun lay down its slope and warmed the rear windows of the overlooking tenements. Before the end of May the caretaker had much ado to keep the growth in order. Vines threatened to engulf the circling street of sepulchers in greenery and bloom, and grass to encroach on the flower plots.

A half century ago there were no rotary lawn-mowers to cut off clover heads; and, if there had been, one could not have been used on these dropping terraces, so populous with slabs and so closely set with turfed mounds and oblongs of early flowering annuals and bedding plants. Mr. Brown had to get down on his hands and knees, with gardener's shears, to clip the turfed borders and banks, and take a sickle to the hummocks. Thus he could dig out a root of dande-

tion with the trowel kept ever in his belt, consider the spreading crocuses and valley lilies,
whether to spare them, give a country violet its
blossoming time, and leave a screening burdock
undisturbed until fledglings were out of their
nests in the shrubbery.

Mistress Jeanie often brought out a little old
milking-stool on balmy mornings, and sat with
knitting or mending in one of the narrow aisles,
to advise her gude-mon in small matters. Bobby
trotted quietly about, sniffing at everything
with the liveliest interest, head on this side or
that, alertly. His business, learned in his first
summer in Greyfriars, was to guard the nests
of foolish skylarks, song-thrushes, redbreasts and
wrens, that built low in lilac, laburnum, and
flowering currant bushes, in crannies of wall and
vault, and on the ground. It cannot but be a
pleasant thing to be a wee young dog, full of life
and good intentions, and to play one's dramatic
part in making an old garden of souls tuneful
with bird song. A cry of alarm from parent or
nestling was answered instantly by the tiny,
tousled policeman, and there was a prowler the
less, or a skulking cat was sent flying over tomb
and wall.

His duty done, without noise or waste of
energy, Bobby returned to lie in the sun on Auld

Jock's grave. Over this beloved mound a cover-
let of rustic turf had been spread as soon as the
frost was out of the ground, and a bonny briar
bush planted at the head. Then it bore nature's
own tribute of flowers, for violets, buttercups,
daisies and clover blossoms opened there and,
later, a spike or so of wild foxglove and a knot
of heather. Robin redbreasts and wrens foraged around Bobby, unafraid; swallows swooped
down from their mud villages, under the dizzy
dormers and gables, to flush the flies on his muzzle,
and whole flocks of little blue titmice fluttered
just overhead, in their rovings from holly and
laurel to newly tasseled firs and yew-trees.

The click of the wicket gate was another sort
of alarm altogether. At that the little dog
slipped under the fallen table-tomb and lay
hidden there until any strange visitor had taken
himself away. Except for two more forced re-
turns and ingenious escapes from the sheep-
farm on the Pentlands, Bobby had lived in the
kirkyard undisturbed for six months. The caretaker had neither the heart to put him out nor
the courage to face the minister and the kirk
officers with a plea for him to remain. The
little dog's presence there was known, apparently, only to Mr. Traill, to a few of the tenement
dwellers. and to the Heriot boys. If his life was

clandestine in a way, it was as regular of hour and
duty and as well ordered as that of the garrison
in the Castle.

When the time-gun boomed, Bobby was let out
for his midday meal at Mr. Traill's and for a
noisy run about the neighborhood to exercise his
lungs and legs. On Wednesdays he haunted the
Grassmarket, sniffing at horses, carts and mired
boots. Edinburgh had so many shaggy little
Skye and Scotch terriers that one more could go
about unremarked. Bobby returned to the kirkyard at his own good pleasure. In the evening
he was given a supper of porridge and broo, or
milk, at the kitchen door of the lodge, and the
nights he spent on Auld Jock's grave. The
morning drum and bugle woke him to the
chase, and all his other hours were spent in close
attendance on the labors of the caretaker. The
click of the wicket gate was the signal for instant
disappearance.

A scramble up the wall from Heriot's Hospital
grounds, or the patter of bare feet on the gravel,
however, was notice to come out and greet a
friend. Bobby was host to the disinherited
children of the tenements. Now, at the tap-tap-
tapping of Tammy Barr's crutches, he scampered
up the slope, and he suited his pace to the
crippled boy's in coming down again. Tammy

chose a heap of cut grass on which to sit en-
throned and play king, a grand new crutch for a
scepter, and Bobby for a courtier. At command,
the little dog rolled over and over, begged, and
walked on his hind legs. He even permitted a
pair of thin little arms to come near strangling
him, in an excess of affection. Then he wagged
his tail and lolled his tongue to show that he was
friendly, and trotted away about his business.
Tammy took an oat-cake from his pocket to
nibble, and began a conversation with Mistress
Jeanie.

"I brocht a picnic wi' me."

"Did ye, noo? An' hoo did ye ken aboot
picnics, laddie?"

"Maister Traill was tellin' Ailie an' me.
There's ilka thing to mak' a picnic i' the kirkyaird. They couldna mak' my legs gude i' the
infairmary, but I'm gangin' to Heriot's. I'll
juist hae to airn ma leevin' wi' ma heid, an' no'
remember aboot ma legs, ava. Is he no' a bonny
doggie?"

"Ay, he's bonny. An' ye're a braw laddie no'
to fash yersel' aboot what canna be helped."

The wifie took his ragged jacket and mended
it, dropped a tear in an impossible hole, and a ha'-
penny in the one good pocket. And by and by
the pale laddie slept there among the bright

graves, in the sun. After another false alarm
from the gate she asked her gude-mon, as she had
asked many times before:

"What 'll ye do, Jamie, when the meenister
kens aboot Bobby, an' ca's ye up afore kirk sessions for brakin' the rule?"

"We wullna cross the brig till we come to the
burn, woman," he invariably answered, with assumed unconcern. Well he knew that the bridge
might be down and the stream in flood when he
came to it. But Mr. Traill was a member of
Greyfriars auld kirk, too, and a companion in
guilt, and Mr. Brown relied not a little on the
landlord's fertile mind and daring tongue. And
he relied on useful, well-behaving Bobby to plead
his own cause.

"There's nae denyin' the doggie is takin' in 'is
ways. He's had twa gude hames fair thrown at
'is heid, but the sperity bit keeps to 'is ain mind.
An' syne he's usefu', an' hauds 'is gab by the
ordinar'." He often reinforced his inclination
with some such argument.

With all their caution, discovery was always
imminent. The kirkyard was long and narrow
and on rising levels, and it was cut almost across
by the low mass of the two kirks, so that many
things might be going on at one end that could
not be seen from the other. On this Saturday

noon, when the Heriot boys were let out for the half-holiday, Mr. Brown kept an eye on them until those who lived outside had dispersed. When Mistress Jeanie tucked her knitting-needles in her belt, and went up to the lodge to put the dinner over the fire, the caretaker went down toward Candlemakers Row to trim the grass about the martyrs' monument. Bobby dutifully trotted at his heels. Almost immediately a half-dozen laddies, led by Geordie Ross and Sandy McGregor, scaled the wall from Heriot's grounds and stepped down into the kirkyard, that lay piled within nearly to the top. They had a perfectly legitimate errand there, but no mission is to be approached directly by romantic boyhood.

"Hist!" was the warning, and the innocent invaders, feeling delightfully lawless, stole over and stormed the marble castle, where "Bluidy" McKenzie slept uneasily against judgment day. Light-hearted lads can do daring deeds on a sunny day that would freeze their blood on a dark and stormy night. So now Geordie climbed nonchalantly to a seat over the old persecutor, crossed his stout, bare legs, filled an imaginary pipe, and rattled the three farthings in his pocket.

"I'm 'Jinglin' Geordie' Heriot," he announced

'I'll show ye hoo a prood goldsmith ance smoked wi' a king."

Then, jauntily: "Sandy, gie a crack to 'Bluidy' McKenzie's door an' daur the auld hornie to come oot."

The deed was done amid breathless apprehensions, but nothing disturbed the silence of the May noon except the lark that sprang at their feet and soared singing into the blue. It was Sandy who presently whistled like a blackbird to attract the attention of Bobby.

There were no blackbirds in the kirkyard, and Bobby understood the signal. He scampered up at once and dashed around the kirk, all excitement, for he had had many adventures with the Heriot boys at skating and hockey on Duddingston Lock in the winter, and tramps over the country and out to Leith harbor in the spring. The laddies prowled along the upper wall of the kirks, opened and shut the wicket, to give the caretaker the idea that they had come in decorously by the gate, and went down to ask him, with due respect and humility, if they could take Bobby out for the afternoon. They were going to mark the places where wild flowers might be had, to decorate "Jinglin' Geordie's" portrait, statue and tomb at the school on Founder's Day.

Mr. Brown considered them with a glower that made the boys nudge each other knowingly. "Saturday isna the day for 'im to be gaen aboot He aye has a washin' an' a groomin' to mak 'im fit for the Sabbath. An', by the leuk o' ye ye'd be nane the waur for soap an' water yer ainsel's."

"We'll gie 'im 'is washin' an' combin' the nicht," they volunteered, eagerly.

"Weel, noo, he wullna hae 'is dinner till the time-gun."

Neither would they. At that, annoyed by their persistence, Mr. Brown denied authority.

"Ye ken weel he isna ma dog. Ye'll hae to gang up an' spier Maister Traill. He's fair daft aboot the gude-for-naethin' tyke."

This was understood as permission. As the boys ran up to the gate, with Bobby at their heels, Mr. Brown called after them: "Ye fetch 'im hame wi' the sunset bugle, an' gin ye teach 'im ony o' yer unmannerly ways I'll tak' a stick to yer breeks."

When they returned to Mr. Traill's place at two o'clock the landlord stood in shirt-sleeves and apron in the open doorway with Bobby, the little dog gripping a mutton shank in his mouth.

"Bobby must tak' his bone down first and hide it awa'. The Sabbath in a kirkyard is a dull day for a wee dog, so he aye gets a catechism of a bone to mumble over."

The landlord sighed in open envy when the laddies and the little dog tumbled down the Row to the Grassmarket on their gypsying. His eyes sought out the glimpse of green country on the dome of Arthur's Seat, that loomed beyond the University towers to the east. There are times when the heart of a boy goes ill with the sordid duties of the man.

Straight down the length of the empty market the laddies ran, through the crooked, fascinating haunt of horses and jockeys in the street of King's Stables, then northward along the fronts of quaint little handicrafts shops that skirted Castle Crag. By turning westward into Queensferry Street a very few minutes would have brought them to a bit of buried country. But every expedition of Edinburgh lads of spirit of that day was properly begun with challenges to scale Castle Rock from the valley park of Princes Street Gardens on the north.

"I daur ye to gang up!" was all that was necessary to set any group of youngsters to scaling the precipice. By every tree and ledge, by every cranny and point of rock, stoutly rooted hazel and thorn bush and clump of gorse, they climbed. These laddies went up a quarter or a

third of the way to the grim ramparts and came
cautiously down again. Bobby scrambled higher,
tumbled back more recklessly and fell, head over
heels and upside down, on the daisied turf. He
righted himself at once, and yelped in sharp protest. Then he sniffed and busied himself with
pretenses, in the elaborate unconcern with which
a little dog denies anything discreditable. There
were legends of daring youth having climbed
this war-like cliff and laying hands on the fortress
wall, but Geordie expressed a popular feeling in
declaring these tales "a' lees."

"No' ony laddie could gang a' the way up an'
come doon wi' 'is heid no' broken. Bobby
couldna do it, an' he's mair like a wild fox than
an ordinar' dog. Noo, we're the Light Brigade
at Balaklava. Chairge!"

The Crimean War was then a recent event.
Heroes of Sebastopol answered the summons of
drum and bugle in the Castle and fired the hearts
of Edinburgh youth. Cannon all around them,
and "theirs not to reason why," this little band
stormed out Queensferry Street and went down,
hand under hand, into the fairy underworld of
Leith Water.

All its short way down from the Pentlands to
the sea, the Water of Leith was then a foaming
little river of mills, twisting at the bottom of a

gorge. One cliff-like wall or the other lay to the sun all day, so that the way was lined with a profusion of every wild thing that turns green and blooms in the Lowlands of Scotland. And it was filled to the brim with bird song and water babble.

A crowd of laddies had only to go inland up this gorge to find wild and tame bloom enough to bury "Jinglin' Geordie" all over again every year. But adventure was to be had in greater variety by dropping seaward with the bickering, brown water. These waded along the shallow margin, walked on shelving sands of gold, and, where the channel was filled, they clung to the rocks and picked their way along dripping ledges. Bobby missed no chance to swim. If he could scramble over rough ground like a squirrel or a fox, he could swim like an otter. Swept over the low dam at Dean village, where a cup-like valley was formed, he tumbled over and over in the spray and was all but drowned. As soon as he got his breath and his bearings he struck out frantically for the bank, shook the foam from his eyes and ears, and barked indignantly at the saucy fall. The white miller in the doorway of the gray-stone, red-roofed mill laughed, and anxious children ran down from a knot of story-book cottages and gay dooryards.

"I'll gie ye ten shullin's for the sperity bit dog," the miller shouted, above the clatter of the wheel and the swish of the dam.

"He isna oor ain dog," Geordie called back. "But he wullna droon. He's got a gude heid to 'im, an' wullna be sic a bittie fule anither time."

Indeed he had a good head on him! Bobby never needed a second lesson. At Silver Mills and Canon Mills he came out and trotted warily around the dam. Where the gorge widened to a valley toward the sea they all climbed up to Leith Walk, that ran to the harbor, and came out to a wonder-world of water-craft anchored in the Firth. Each boy picked out his ship to go adventuring.

"I'm gangin' to Norway!"

Geordie was scornful. "Hoots, ye tame pussies. Ye're fleid o' gettin' yer feet wat. I'll be rinnin' aff to be a pirate. Come awa' doon."

They followed the leader along shore and boarded an abandoned and evil-smelling fishing-boat. There they ran up a ragged jacket for a black flag. But sailing a stranded craft palled presently.

"Nae, I'm gangin' to be a Crusoe. Preserve me! If there's no' a futprint i' the sand! Bobby's ma sma' man Friday."

Away they ran southward to find a castaway's

shelter in a hollow on the golf links. Soon this was transformed into a wrecker's den, and then into the hiding-place of a harried Covenanter fleeing religious persecution. Daring things to do swarmed in upon their minds, for Edinburgh laddies live in a city of romantic history, of soldiers, of near-by mountains, and of sea-rovings. No adventure served them five minutes, and Bobby was in every one. Ah, lucky Bobby, to have such gay playfellows on a sunny afternoon and under foot the open country!

And fortunate laddies to have such a merry rascal of a wee dog with them! To the mile they ran, Bobby went five, scampering in wide circles and barking and louping at butterflies and whaups. He made a detour to the right to yelp saucily at the red-coated sentry who paced before the Gothic gateway to the deserted Palace of Holyrood, and as far to the left to harry the hoofs of a regiment of cavalry drilling before the barracks at Piershill. He raced on ahead and swam out to scatter the fleet of swan sailing on the blue mirror of Duddingston Loch.

The tired boys lay blissfully up the sunny side of Arthur's Seat in a thicket of hazel while Geordie carried out a daring plan for which privacy was needed. Bobby was solemnly arraigned before a court on the charge of being a

seditious Covenanting meenister, and was required
to take the oath of loyalty to English King and
Church on pain of being hanged in the Grassmarket. The oath had been duly written out on
paper and greased with mutton tallow to make
it more palatable. Bobby licked the fat off with
relish. Then he took the paper between his
sharp little teeth and merrily tore it to shreds.
And, having finished it, he barked cheerful defiance at the court. The lads came near rolling
down the slope with laughter, and they gave three
cheers for the little hero. Sandy remarked:

"Ye wadna think, noo, sic a sonsie doggie wad
be leevin' i' the murky auld kirkyaird."

Bobby had learned the lay of the tipped-up and
scooped-out and jumbled auld toon, and he led
the way homeward along the southern outskirts
of the city. He turned up Nicolson Street, that
ran northward, past the University and the old
infirmary. To get into Greyfriars Place from
the east at that time one had to descend to the
Cowgate and climb out again. Bobby darted
down the first of the narrow wynds.

Suddenly he turned 'round and 'round in bewilderment, then shot through a sculptured doorway, into a well-like court, and up a flight of stone
stairs. The slamming of a shutter overhead
shocked him to a standstill on the landing and

sent him dropping slowly down again. What memories surged back to his little brain, what grief gripped his heart, as he stood trembling on a certain spot in the pavement where once a long deal box had rested!

"What ails the bittie dog?" There was something here that sobered the thoughtless boys. "Come awa', Bobby!"

At that he came obediently enough. But he trotted down the very middle of the wynd, head and tail low, and turned unheeding into the Saturday-evening roar of the Cowgate. He refused to follow them up the rise between St. Magdalen's Chapel and the eastern parapet of the bridge, but kept to his way under the middle arch into the Grassmarket. By way of Candlemakers Row he gained the kirkyard gate, and when the wicket was opened he disappeared around the church. When Bobby failed to answer calls, Mr. Brown grumbled, but went after him. The little dog submitted to his vigorous scrubbing and grooming, but he refused his supper. Without a look or a wag of the tail he was gone again.

"Noo, what hae ye done to 'im? He's no' like 'is ainsel' ava."

They had done nothing, indeed. They could only relate Bobby's strange behavior in College

Wynd and the rest of the way home. Mistress Jeanie nodded her head, with the wisdom of women that is of the heart.

"Eh, Jamie, that wad be whaur 'is maister deed sax months syne." And having said it she slipped down the slope with her knitting and sat on the mound beside the mourning little dog.

When the awe-struck lads asked for the story Mr. Brown shook his head. "Ye spier Maister Traill. He kens a' aboot it; an' syne he can talk like a beuk."

Before they left the kirkyard the laddies walked down to Auld Jock's grave and patted Bobby on the head, and they went away thoughtfully to their scattered homes.

As on that first morning when his grief was new, Bobby woke to a Calvinistic Sabbath. There were no rattling carts or hawkers crying their wares. Steeped in sunshine, the Castle loomed golden into the blue. Tenement dwellers slept late, and then moved about quietly. Children with unwontedly clean faces came out to galleries and stairs to study their catechisms. Only the birds were unaware of the seventh day, and went about their melodious business; and flower buds opened to the sun.

In mid-morning there suddenly broke on the sweet stillness that clamor of discordant bells

that made the wayfarer in Edinburgh stop his
ears. All the way from Leith Harbor to the
Burghmuir eight score of warring bells con-
tended to be heard. Greyfriars alone was silent
in that babblement, for it had lost tower and bell
in an explosion of gunpowder. And when the
din ceased at last there was a sound of military
music. The Castle gates swung wide, and a
kilted regiment marched down High Street
playing "God Save the Queen." When Bobby
was in good spirits the marching music got
into his legs and set him to dancing scandal-
ously. The caretaker and his wifie always
came around the kirk on pleasant mornings to
see the bonny sight of the gay soldiers going to
church.

To wee Bobby these good, comfortable, every-
day friends of his must have seemed strange in
their black garments and their serious Sunday
faces. And, ah! the Sabbath must, indeed, have
been a dull day to the little dog. He had learned
that when the earliest comer clicked the wicket
he must go under the table-tomb and console
himself with the extra bone that Mr. Traill never
failed to remember. With an hour's respite for
dinner at the lodge, between the morning and
afternoon services, he lay there all day. The
restaurant was closed, and there was no running

about for good dogs. In the early dark of winter he could come out and trot quietly about the silent, deserted place.

As soon as the crocuses pushed their green noses through the earth in the spring the congregation began to linger among the graves, for to see an old burying-ground renew its life is a peculiar promise of the resurrection. By midsummer visitors were coming from afar, some even from over-sea, to read the quaint inscriptions on the old tombs, or to lay tributes of flowers on the graves of poets and religious heroes. It was not until the late end of such a day that Bobby could come out of hiding to stretch his cramped legs. Then it was that tenement children dropped from low windows, over the tombs, and ate their suppers of oat-cake there in the fading light.

When Mr. Traill left the kirkyard in the bright evening of the last Sunday in May he stopped without to wait for Dr. Lee, the minister of Greyfriars auld kirk, who had been behind him to the gate. Now he was nowhere to be seen. With Bobby ever in the background of his mind, at such times of possible discovery, Mr. Traill reentered the kirkyard. The minister was sitting on the fallen slab, tall silk hat off, with Mr. Brown standing beside him, uncovered and miserable of aspect, and Bobby looking up anxiously at this new element in his fate.

"Do you think it seemly for a dog to be living in the churchyard, Mr. Brown?" The minister's voice was merely kind and inquiring, but the caretaker was in fault, and this good English was disconcerting. However, his conscience acquitted him of moral wrong, and his sturdy Scotch independence came to the rescue.

"Gin a bit dog, wha hauds 'is gab, isna seemly, thae pussies are the deil's ain bairns."

The minister lifted his hand in rebuke. "Remember the Sabbath Day. And I see no cats, Mr. Brown."

"Ye wullna see ony as lang as the wee doggie is leevin' i' the kirkyaird. An' the vermin hae sneekit awa' the first time sin' Queen Mary's day. An' syne there's mair singin' birdies than for mony a year."

Mr. Traill had listened, unseen. Now he came forward with a gay challenge in broad Scotch to put the all but routed caretaker at his ease.

"Doctor, I hae a queistion to spier ye. Which is mair unseemly: a weel-behavin' bittie tyke i' the kirkyaird or a scandalous organ i' the kirk?"

"Ah, Mr. Traill, I'm afraid you're a sad, irreverent young dog yourself, sir." The minister

broke into a genial laugh. "Man, you've spoiled
a bit of fun I was having with Mr. Brown, who
takes his duties 'sairiously.'" He sat looking
down at the little dog until Bobby came up to
him and stood confidingly under his caressing
hand. Then he added: "I have suspected for
some months that he was living in the churchyard. It is truly remarkable that an active,
noisy little Skye could keep so still about it."

At that Mr. Brown retreated to the martyrs'
monument to meditate on the unministerial behavior of this minister and professor of Biblical
criticism in the University. Mr. Traill, however,
sat himself down on the slab for a pleasant
probing into the soul of this courageous dominie,
who had long been under fire for his innovations
in the kirk services.

"I heard of Bobby first early in the winter, from
a Bible-reader at the Medical Mission in the
Cowgate, who saw the little dog's master buried.
He sees many strange, sad things in his work, but
nothing ever shocked him so as the lonely death
of that pious old shepherd in such a picturesque
den of vice and misery."

"Ay, he went from my place, fair ill, into the
storm. I never knew whaur the auld man died."

The minister looked at Mr. Traill, struck by
the note of remorse in his tone.

"The missionary returned to the churchyard to look for the dog that had refused to leave the grave. He concluded that Bobby had gone away to a new home and master, as most dogs do go sooner or later. Some weeks afterward the minister of a small church in the hills inquired for him and insisted that he was still here. This last week, at the General Assembly, I heard of the wee Highlander from several sources. The tales of his escapes from the sheep-farm have grown into a sort of Odyssey of the Pentlands. I think, perhaps, if you had not continued to feed him, Mr. Traill, he might have remained at his old home."

"Nae, I'm no' thinking so, and I was no' willing to risk the starvation of the bonny, leal Highlander."

Until the stars came out Mr. Traill sat there telling the story. At mention of his master's name Bobby returned to the mound and stretched himself across it. "I will go before the kirk officers, Doctor Lee, and tak' full responseebility. Mr. Brown is no' to blame. It would have tak'n a man with a heart of trap-rock to have turned the woeful bit dog out."

"He is well cared for and is of a hardy breed, so he is not likely to suffer; but a dog, no more than a man, cannot live on bread alone. His heart hungers for love."

"Losh!" cried Mr. Brown. "Are ye thinkin'
he isna gettin' it? Oor bairns are a' oot o' the
hame nest, an' ma woman, Jeanie, is fair daft
aboot Bobby, aye thinkin' he'll tak' the measles.
An' syne, there's a' the tenement bairns cryin'
oot on 'im ilka meenit, an' ane crippled laddie
he e'en lets fondle 'im."

"Still, it would be better if he belonged to
some one master. Everybody's dog is nobody's
dog," the minister insisted. "I wish you could
attach him to you, Mr. Traill."

"Ay, it's a disappointment to me that he'll
no' bide with me. Perhaps, in time—"

"It's nae use, ava," Mr. Brown interrupted,
and he related the incident of the evening before.
"He's cheerfu' eneugh maist o' the time, an' likes
to be wi' the laddies as weel as ony dog, but he
isna forgettin' Auld Jock. The wee doggie cam'
again to 'is maister's buryin'. Man, ye ne'er
saw the like o' it. The wifie found 'im flattened
oot to a furry door-mat, an' greetin' to brak 'is
heart."

"It's a remarkable story; and he's a beautiful
little dog, and a leal one." The minister stooped
and patted Bobby, and he was thoughtful all the
way to the gate.

"The matter need not be brought up in any
formal way. I will speak to the elders and

deacons about it privately, and refer those wanting details to you, Mr. Traill. Mr. Brown," he
called to the caretaker who stood in the lodge
door, "it cannot be pleasing to God to see the
little creature restrained. Give Bobby his liberty on the Sabbath

IT was more than eight years after Auld Jock fled from the threat of a doctor that Mr. Traill's prediction, that his tongue would get him into trouble with the magistrates, was fulfilled; and then it was because of the least-considered slip in speaking to a boyhood friend who happened to be a Burgh policeman.

Many things had tried the landlord of Ye Olde Greyfriars Dining-Rooms. After a series of soft April days, in which lilacs budded and birds sang in the kirkyard, squalls of wind and rain came up out of the sea-roaring east. The smoky old town of Edinburgh was so shaken and beaten upon and icily drenched that rattling finials and tiles were torn from ancient gables and whirled abroad. Rheumatic pains were driven into the joints of the elderly. Mr. Brown took to his bed in the lodge, and Mr. Traill was touchy in his temper.

A sensitive little dog learns to read the human barometer with a degree of accuracy rarely attained by fellowmen and, in times of low pressure, wisely effaces himself. His rough thatch streaming, Bobby trotted in blithely for his dinner, ate it under the settle, shook himself dry, and dozed half the afternoon.

To the casual observer the wee terrier was no older than when his master died. As swift of foot and as sound of wind as he had ever been, he could tear across country at the heels of a new generation of Heriot laddies and be as fresh as a daisy at nightfall. Silvery gray all over, the whitening hairs on his face and tufted feet were not visible. His hazel-brown eyes were still as bright and soft and deep as the sunniest pools of Leith Water. It was only when he opened his mouth for a tiny, pink cavern of a yawn that the points of his teeth could be seen to be wearing down; and his after-dinner nap was more prolonged than of old. At such times Mr. Traill recalled that the longest life of a dog is no more than a fifth of the length of days allotted to man.

On that snarling April day, when only himself and the flossy ball of sleeping Skye were in the place, this thought added to Mr. Traill's discontent. There had been few guests. Those who had come in, soaked and surly, ate their dinner in silence and discomfort and took themselves away, leaving the freshly scrubbed floor as mucky as a moss-hag on the moor. Late in the afternoon a sergeant, risen from the ranks and cocky about it, came in and turned himself out of a dripping greatcoat, dapper and dry in his red tunic, pipe-clayed belt, and winking buttons. He ordered tea and toast and Dundee marmalade with an air of gay well-being that was no less than a personal affront to a man in Mr. Traill's frame of mind. Trouble brewed with the tea that Ailie Lindsey, a tall lassie of fifteen, but shy and elfish as of old, brought in on a tray from the scullery.

When this spick-and-span non-commissioned officer demanded Mr. Traill's price for the little dog that took his eye, the landlord replied curtly that Bobby was not for sale. The soldier was insolently amused.

"That's vera surprisin'. I aye thoucht an Edinburgh shopkeeper wad sell ilka thing he had, an' tak' the siller to bed wi' 'im to keep 'im snug the nicht."

Mr. Traill returned, with brief sarcasm, that "his lairdship" had been misinformed.

"Why wull ye no' sell the bit dog?" the man insisted.

The badgered landlord turned upon him and answered at length, after the elaborate manner of a minister who lays his sermon off in sections

"First: he's no' my dog to sell. Second: he'

a dog of rare discreemination, and is no' like to tak' you for a master. Third: you soldiers aye have with you a special brand of shulling-a-day impudence. And, fourth and last, my brither: I'm no' needing your siller, and I can manage to do fair weel without your conversation."

As this bombardment proceeded, the sergeant's jaw dropped. When it was finished he laughed heartily and slapped his knee. "Man, come an' brak bread wi' me or I'll hae to brak yer stiff neck."

A truce was declared over a cozy pot of tea, and the two became at least temporary friends. It was such a day that the landlord would have gossiped with a gaol-bird; and when a soldier who has seen years of service, much of it in strange lands, once admits a shopkeeper to equality, he can be affable and entertaining "by the ordinar'." Mr. Traill sketched Bobby's story broadly, and to a sympathetic listener; and the soldier told the landlord of the animals that had lived and died in the Castle.

Parrots and monkeys and strange dogs and cats had been brought there by regiments returning from foreign countries and colonies. But most of the pets had been native dogs— collies, spaniels and terriers, and animals of mixed breeds and of no breed at all, but just good dogs. No one knew when the custom began, but there was an old and well-filled cemetery for the Castle pets. When a dog died a little stone was set up, with the name of the animal and the regiment to which it had belonged on it. Soldiers often went there among the tiny mounds and told stories of the virtues and taking ways of old favorites. And visitors read the names of Flora and Guy and Dandie, of Prince Charlie and Rob Roy, of Jeanie and Bruce and Wattie. It was a merry life for a dog in the Castle. He was petted and spoiled by homesick men, and when he died there were a thousand mourners at his funeral.

"Put it to the bit Skye noo. If he tak's the Queen's shullin' he belongs to the army." The sergeant flipped a coin before Bobby, who was wagging his tail and sniffing at the military boots with his ever lively interest in soldiers.

He looked up at the tossed coin indifferently, and when it fell to the floor he let it lie. "Siller" has no meaning to a dog. His love can be purchased with nothing less than his chosen master's heart. The soldier sighed at Bobby's indifference. He introduced himself as Sergeant Scott, of the Royal Engineers, detailed from headquarters to direct the work in the

Castle crafts shops. Engineers rank high **in** pay and in consideration, and it was no ordinary Jack of all trades who had expert knowledge of so many skilled handicrafts. Mr. Traill's respect and liking for the man increased with the passing moments.

As the sergeant departed he warned Mr. Traill, laughingly, that he meant to kidnap Bobby the very first chance he got. The Castle pet had died, and Bobby was altogether too good a dog to be wasted on a moldy auld kirkyard and thrown on a dust-cart when he came to die.

Mr. Traill resented the imputation. "He'll no' be thrown on a dust-cart!"

The door was shut on the mocking retort: "Hoo do ye ken he wullna?"

And there was food for gloomy reflection. The landlord could not know, in truth, what Bobby's ultimate fate might be. But little over nine years of age, he should live only five or six years longer at most. Of his friends, Mr. Brown was ill and aging, and might have to give place to a younger man. He himself was in his prime, but he could not be certain of living longer than this hardy little dog. For the first time he realized the truth of Dr. Lee's saying that everybody's dog was nobody's dog. The tenement children held Bobby in a sort of community affection.

He was the special pet of the Heriot laddies, but a class was sent into the world every year and was scattered far. Not one of all the hundreds of bairns who had known and loved this little dog could give him any real care or protection.

For the rest, Bobby had remained almost un- known. Many of the congregations of old and new Greyfriars had never seen or heard of him. When strangers were about he seemed to prefer lying in his retreat under the fallen tomb. His Sunday-afternoon naps he usually took in the lodge kitchen. And so, it might very well happen that his old age would be friendless, that he would come to some forlorn end, and be carried away on the dustman's cart. It might, indeed, be better for him to end his days in love and honor in the Castle. But to this solution of the problem Mr. Traill himself was not reconciled.

Sensing some shifting of the winds in the man's soul, Bobby trotted over to lick his hand. Then he sat up on the hearth and lolled his tongue, re- minding the good landlord that he had one cheerful friend to bear him company on the blaw-weary day. It was thus they sat, compan- ionably, when a Burgh policeman who was well known to Mr. Traill came in to dry himself by the fire. Gloomy thoughts were dispelled at once by the instinct of hospitality.

"You're fair wet, man. Pull a chair to the hearth. And you have a bit smut on your nose, Davie."

"It's frae the railway engine. Edinburgh was a reekie toon eneugh afore the engines cam' in an' belched smuts in ilka body's faces." The policeman was disgusted and discouraged by three days of wet clothing, and he would have to go out into the rain again before he got dry. Nothing occurred to him to talk about but grievances.

"Did ye ken the Laird Provost, Maister Chambers, is intendin' to knock a lang hole aboon the tap o' the Coogate wynds? It wull mak' a braid street ye can leuk doon frae yer doorway here. The gude auld days gangin' doon in a muckle dust!"

"Ay, the sun will peep into foul places it hasn't seen sin' Queen Mary's day. And, Davie, it would be more according to the gude auld customs you're so fond of to call Mr. William Chambers 'Glenormiston' for his bit country place."

"He's no' a laird."

"Nae; but he'll be a laird the next time the Queen shows her bonny face north o' the Tweed. Tak' 'a cup o' kindness' with me, man. Hot tay will tak' the cauld out of your disposeetion."

Mr. Traill pulled a bell-cord and Ailie, unused as yet to bells, put her startled little face in at the door to the scullery. At sight of the police-man she looked more than ever like a scared rabbit, and her hands shook when she set the tray down before him. A tenement child grew up in an atmosphere of hostility to uniformed authority, which seldom appeared except to inter-fere with what were considered personal affairs.

The tea mollified the dour man, but there was one more rumbling. "I'm no' denyin' the Provost's gude-hearted. Ance he got up a hame for gaen-aboot dogs, an' he had naethin' to mak' by that. But he canna keep 'is spoon oot o' ilka body's porridge. He's fair daft to tear doon the wa's that cut St. Giles up into fower, snod, white kirks, an' mak' it the ane muckle kirk it was in auld Papist days. There are folk that say, gin he doesna leuk oot, anither kale wifie wull be throwin' a bit stool at 'is meddlin' heid."

"Eh, nae doubt. There's aye a plentifu' supply o' fules in the warld."

Seeing his good friend so well entertained, and needing his society no longer, Bobby got up, wagged his tail in farewell, and started toward the door. Mr. Traill summoned the little maid and spoke to her kindly: "Give Bobby a bone, lassie, and then open the door for him."

In carrying out these instructions Ailie gave the policeman as wide leeway as possible and kept a wary eye upon him. The officer's duties were chiefly up on High Street. He seldom crossed the bridge, and it happened that he had never seen Bobby before. Just by way of making conversation he remarked, "I didna ken ye had a dog, John."

Ailie stopped stock still, the cups on the tray she was taking out tinkling from her agitation. It was thus policemen spoke at private doors in the dark tenements: "I didna ken ye had the smallpox." But Mr. Traill seemed in no way alarmed. He answered with easy indulgence: "That's no' surprising. There's mony a thing you dinna ken, Davie."

The landlord forgot the matter at once, but Ailie did not, for she saw the officer flush darkly and, having no answer ready, go out in silence. In truth, the good-humored sarcasm rankled in the policeman's breast. An hour later he suddenly came to a standstill below the clock tower of the Tron kirk on High Street, and he chuckled.

"Eh, John Traill. Ye're unco' weel furnished i' the heid, but there's ane or twa things ye dinna ken yer ainsel'."

Entirely taken up with his brilliant idea, he lost no time in putting it to work. He dodged among the standing cabs and around the buttresses of St. Giles that projected into the thoroughfare. In the mid-century there was a police office in the middle of the front of the historic old cathedral that had then fallen to its lowest ebb of fortune. There the officer reported a matter that was strictly within the line of his duty.

Very early the next morning he was standing before the door of Mr. Traill's place, in the fitful sunshine of clearing skies, when the landlord appeared to begin the business of the day.

"Are ye Maister John Traill?"

"Havers, Davie! What ails you, man? You know my name as weel as you know your ain."

"It's juist a formality o' the law to mak' ye admit yer identity. Here's a bit paper for ye." He thrust an official-looking document into Mr. Traill's hand and took himself away across the bridge, fair satisfied with his conduct of an affair of subtlety.

It required five minutes for Mr. Traill to take in the import of the legal form. Then a wrathful explosion vented itself on the unruly key that persisted in dodging the keyhole. But once within he read the paper again, put it away thoughtfully in an inner pocket, and outwardly subsided to his ordinary aspect. He despatched the business of the day with unusual attention to details and courtesy to guests, and when, in mid-afternoon, the place was empty, he followed Bobby to the kirkyard and inquired at the lodge if he could see Mr. Brown.

"He isna so ill, noo, Maister Traill, but I wadna advise ye to hae muckle to say to 'im." Mistress Jeanie wore the arch look of the wifie who is somewhat amused by a convalescent husband's ill humors. "The pains grupped 'im sair, an' noo that he's easier he'd see us a' hanged wi' pleesure. Is it onything by the ordinar'?"

"Nae. It's just a sma' matter I can attend to my ainsel'. Do you think he could be out the morn?"

"No' afore a week or twa, an' syne, gin the bonny sun comes oot to bide a wee."

Mr. Traill left the kirkyard and went out to George Square to call upon the minister of Greyfriars auld kirk. The errand was unfruitful, and he was back in ten minutes, to spend the evening alone, without even the consolation of Bobby's company, for the little dog was unhappy outside the kirkyard after sunset. And he took an unsettling thought to bed with him.

Here was a pretty kettle of fish, indeed, for a respected member of a kirk and middle-aged business man to fry in. Through the legal

verbiage Mr. Traill made out that he was sum‑
moned to appear before whatever magistrate
happened to be sitting on the morrow in the
Burgh court, to answer to the charge of owning,
or harboring, one dog, upon which he had not
paid the license tax of seven shillings.

For all its absurdity it was no laughing matter.
The municipal court of Edinburgh was of far
greater dignity than the ordinary justice court of
the United Kingdom and of America.   The civic
bench was occupied, in turn, by no less a personage
than the Lord Provost as chief, and by five other
magistrates elected by the Burgh council from
among its own membership.   Men of standing in
business, legal and University circles, considered
it an honor and a duty to bring their knowledge
and responsibility to bear on the pettiest police
cases.

It was morning before Mr. Traill had the
glimmer of an idea to take with him on this
unlucky business.   An hour before the opening
of court he crossed the bridge into High Street,
which was then as picturesquely Gothic and
decaying and overpopulated as the Cowgate,
but high-set, wind-swept and sun-searched, all
the way up the sloping mile from Holyrood Pal‑
ace to the Castle.   The ridge fell away steeply,
through rifts of wynds and closes, to the Cow‑

gate ravine on the one hand, and to Princes Street's parked valley on the other. Mr. Traill turned into the narrow descent of Warriston Close. Little more than a crevice in the precipice of tall, old buildings, on it fronted a business house whose firm name was known wherever the English language was read: "W. and R. Chambers, Publishers."

From top to bottom the place was gas-lit, even on a sunny spring morning, and it hummed and clattered with printing-presses. No one was in the little anteroom to the editorial offices beside a young clerk, but at sight of a red-headed, freckle-faced Heriot laddie of Bobby's puppyhood days Mr. Traill's spirits rose.

"A gude day to you, Sandy McGregor; and whaur's your auld twin conspirator, Geordie Ross?"

"He's a student in the Medical College, Mr. Traill. He went by this meenit to the Botanical Garden for herbs my grandmither has aye known without books." Sandy grinned in appreciation of this foolishness, but he added, with Scotch shrewdness, "It's gude for the book-prenting beesiness."

"It is so," the landlord agreed, heartily. "But you must no' be forgetting that the Chambers brothers war book readers and sellers before they war publishers. You are weel set up in life, laddie, and Heriot's has pulled the warst of the burrs from your tongue. I'm wanting to see Glenormiston."

"Mr. William Chambers is no' in. Mr. Robert is aye in, but he's no' liking to be fashed about sma' things."

"I'll no' trouble him. It's the Lord Provost I'm wanting, on ofeecial beesiness." He requested Sandy to ask Glenormiston, if he came in, to come over to the Burgh court and spier for Mr. Traill.

"It's no' his day to sit as magistrate, and he's no' like to go unless it's a fair sairious matter."

"Ay, it is, laddie. It's a matter of life and death, I'm thinking!" He smiled grimly, as it entered his head that he might be driven to do violence to that meddling policeman. The yellow gas-light gave his face such a sardonic aspect that Sandy turned pale.

"Wha's death, man?"

Mr. Traill kept his own counsel, but at the door he turned: "You'll no' be remembering the bittie terrier that lived in the kirkyard?"

The light of boyhood days broke in Sandy's grin. "Ay, I'll no' be forgetting the sonsie tyke. He was a deil of a dog to tak' on a holiday. Is he still faithfu' to his dead master?"

"He is that; and for his faithfu'ness he's like to be dead himsel'. The police are takin' up masterless dogs an' putting them out o' the way. I'll mak' a gude fight for Bobby in the Burgh court."

"I'll fight with you, man." The spirit of the McGregor clan, though much diluted and subdued by town living, brought Sandy down from a three-legged stool. He called another clerk to take his place, and made off to find the Lord Provost, powerful friend of hameless dogs. Mr. Traill hastened down to the Royal Exchange, below St. Giles and on the northern side of High Street.

Less than a century old, this municipal building was modern among ancient rookeries. To High Street it presented a classic front of four stories, recessed by flanking wings, around three sides of a quadrangular courtyard. Near the entrance there was a row of barber shops and coffee-rooms. Any one having business with the city offices went through a corridor between these places of small trade to the stairway court behind them. On the floor above, one had to inquire of some uniformed attendant in which of the oaken, ante-roomed halls the Burgh court was sitting. And by the time one got there all the pride of civic history of the ancient royal

Burgh, as set forth in portrait and statue and a museum of antiquities, was apt to take the lime out of the backbone of a man less courageous than Mr. Traill. What a car of Juggernaut to roll over one, small, masterless terrier!

But presently the landlord found himself on his feet, and not so ill at ease. A Scottish court, high or low, civil or criminal, had a flavor all its own. Law points were threshed over with gusto, but counsel, client, and witness gained many a point by ready wit, and there was no lack of dry humor from the bench. About the Burgh court, for all its stately setting, there was little formality. The magistrate of the day sat behind a tall desk, with a clerk of record at his elbow, and the officer gave his testimony briefly: Edinburgh being quite overrun by stray and unlicensed dogs, orders had recently been given the Burgh police to report such animals. In Mr. Traill's place he had seen a small terrier that appeared to be at home there; and, indeed, on the dog's going out, Mr. Traill had called a servant lassie to fetch a bone, and to open the door for him. He noticed that the animal wore no collar, and felt it his duty to report the matter.

By the time Mr. Traill was called to answer to the charge a number of curious idlers had gathered on the back benches. He admitted his name and address, but denied that he either owned or was harboring a dog. The magistrate fixed a cold eye upon him, and asked if he meant to contradict the testimony of the officer.

"Nae, your Honor; and he might have seen the same thing ony week-day of the past eight and a half years. But the bit terrier is no' my ain dog." Suddenly, the memory of the stormy night, the sick old man and the pathos of his renunciation of the only beating heart in the world that loved him—"Bobby isna ma ain dog!"—swept over the remorseful landlord. He was filled with a fierce championship of the wee Highlander, whose loyalty to that dead master had brought him to this strait.

To the magistrate Mr. Traill's tossed-up head had the effect of defiance, and brought a sharp rebuke. "Don't split hairs, Mr. Traill. You are wasting the time of the court. You admit feeding the dog. Who is his master and where does he sleep?"

"His master is in his grave in auld Greyfriars kirkyard, and the dog has aye slept there on the mound."

The magistrate leaned over his desk. "Man, no dog could sleep in the open for one winter in this climate. Are you fond of romancing, Mr. Traill?"

"No' so overfond, your Honor. The dog is o\
the subarctic breed of Skye terriers, the kind
with a thick under-jacket of fleece, and a weather
thatch that turns rain like a crofter's cottage
roof."

"There should be witnesses to such an extraordinary story. The dog could not have
lived in this strictly guarded churchyard without
the consent of those in authority." The magistrate was plainly annoyed and skeptical, and
Mr. Traill felt the sting of it.

"Ay, the caretaker has been his gude friend,
but Mr. Brown is ill of rheumatism, and can no'
come out. Nae doubt, if necessary, his deposee-
tion could be tak'n. Permission for the bit dog
to live in the kirkyard was given by the meenister
of Greyfriars auld kirk, but Doctor Lee is in
failing health and has gone to the south of
France. The tenement children and the Heriot
laddies have aye made a pet of Bobby, but they
would no' be competent witnesses."

"You should have counsel. There are some
legal difficulties here."

"I'm no' needing a lawyer. The law in sic a
matter can no' be so complicated, and I have a
tongue in my ain head that has aye served me,
your Honor." The magistrate smiled, and the
spectators moved to the nearer benches to enjoy

this racy man. The room began to fill by that kind of telepathy that causes crowds to gather around the human drama. One man stood, unnoticed, in the doorway. Mr. Traill went on, quietly: "If the court permits me to do so, I shall be glad to pay for Bobby's license, but I'm thinking that carries responsibeelity for the bit dog."

"You are quite right, Mr. Traill. You would have to assume responsibility. Masterless dogs have become a serious nuisance in the city."

"I could no' tak' responsibeelity. The dog is no' with me more than a couple of hours out of the twenty-four. I understand that most of his time is spent in the kirkyard, in weel-behaving, usefu' ways, but I could no' be sure."

"But why have you fed him for so many years? Was his master a friend?"

"Nae, just a customer, your Honor; a simple auld shepherd who ate his market-day dinner in my place. He aye had the bit dog with him, and I was the last man to see the auld body before he went awa' to his meeserable death in a Cowgate wynd. Bobby came to me, near starved, to be fed, two days after his master's burial. I was tak'n by the wee Highlander's leal spirit."

And that was all the landlord would say. He

had no mind to wear his heart upon his sleeve for this idle crowd to gape at.

After a moment the magistrate spoke warmly: "It appears, then, that the payment of the license could not be accepted from you. Your humanity is commendable, Mr. Traill, but technically you are in fault. The minimum fine should be imposed and remitted."

At this utterly unlooked-for conclusion Mr. Traill seemed to gather his lean shoulders together for a spring, and his gray eyes narrowed to blades.

"With due respect to your Honor, I must tak' an appeal against sic a deceesion, to the Lord Provost and a' the magistrates, and then to the Court of Sessions."

"You would get scant attention, Mr. Traill. The higher judiciary have more important business than reviewing dog cases. You would be laughed out of court."

The dry tone stung him to instant retort. "And in gude company I'd be. Fifty years syne Lord Erskine was laughed down in Parliament for proposing to give legal protection to dumb animals. But we're getting a bit more ceevilized."

"Tut, tut, Mr. Traill, you are making far too much of a small matter."

"It's no' a sma' matter to be entered in the

GREYFRIARS BOBBY

records of the Burgh court as a petty law-braker
And if I continued to feed the dog I would be in
contempt of court."

The magistrate was beginning to feel badgered.
"The fine carries the interdiction with it, Mr.
Traill, if you are asking for information."

"It was no' for information, but just to mak'
plain my ain line of conduct. I'm no' intending
to abandon the dog. I am commended here for
my humanity, but the bit dog I must let starve
for a technicality."

Instantly, as the magistrate half rose from the
bench, the landlord saw that he had gone too far,
and put the court on the defensive. In an easy,
conversational tone, as if unaware of the point
he had scored, he asked if he might address his
accuser on a personal matter. "We knew each
other weel as laddies. Davie, when you're in my
neeborhood again on a wet day, come in and dry
yoursel' by my fire and tak' another cup o' kindness for auld lang syne. You'll be all the better
man for a lesson in morals the bit dog can give
you: no' to bite the hand that feeds you."

The policeman turned purple. A ripple of
merriment ran through the room. The magistrate put his hand up to his mouth, and the clerk
began to drop pens. Before silence was restored
a messenger laddie ran up with a note for the

bench. The magistrate read it with a look of relief, and nodded to the man who had been listening from the doorway, but who disappeared at once.

"The case is ordered continued. The defendant will be given time to secure witnesses, and notified when to appear. The next case is called."

Somewhat dazed by this sudden turn, and annoyed by the delayed settlement of the affair, Mr. Traill hastened from the court-room. As he gained the street he was overtaken by the messenger with a second note. And there was a still more surprising turn that sent the landlord off up swarming High Street, across the bridge, and on to his snug little place of business, with the face and the heart of a school-boy. When Bobby, draggled by three days of wet weather, came in for his dinner, Mr. Traill scanned him critically and in some perplexity. At the end of the day's work, as Ailie was dropping her quaint curtsy and giving her adored employer a shy "gude nicht," he had a sudden thought that made him call her back.

"Did you ever give a bit dog a washing, lassie?"

"Ye mean Bobby, Maister Traill? Nae, I didna." Her eyes sparkled. "But Tammy's hauded 'im for Maister Brown, an' he says it's sonsie to gie the bonny wee a washin'.''

"Weel, Mr. Brown is fair ill, and there has been foul weather. Bobby's getting to look like a poor 'gaen-aboot' dog. Have him at the kirk-yard gate at a quarter to eight o'clock the morn looking like a leddy's pet and I'll dance a Highland fling at your wedding."

"Are ye gangin' to tak' Bobby on a picnic, Maister Traill?"

He answered with a mock solemnity and a twinkle in his eyes that mystified the little maid. ''Nae, lassie; I'm going to tak' him to a meeting in a braw kirk."

IX

WHEN Ailie wanted to get up unusually early in the morning she made use of Tammy for an alarm-clock. A crippled laddie who must "mak' 'is leevin' wi' 'is heid" can waste no moment of daylight, and in the ancient buildings around Greyfriars the maximum of daylight was to be had only by those able and willing to climb to the gables. Tammy, having to live on the lowest, darkest floor of all, used the kirkyard for a study, by special indulgence of the caretaker, whenever the weather permitted.

From a window he dropped his books and his crutches over the wall. Then, by clasping his arms around a broken shaft that blocked the casement, he swung himself out, and scrambled down into an enclosed vault-yard. There he kept hidden Mistress Jeanie's milking-stool for a seat; and a table-tomb served as well, for the laddie to do his sums upon, as it had for the tearful signing of the Covenant more than two hundred years before. Bobby, as host, greeted Tammy with cordial friskings and waggings, saw him settled to

nis tasks, and then went briskly about his own
interrupted business of searching out marauders.
Many a spring dawn the quiet little boy and the
swift and silent little dog had the shadowy garden all to themselves, and it was for them the
song - thrushes and skylarks gave their choicest
concerts.

On that mid-April morning, when the rising sun
gilded the Castle turrets and flashed back from
the many beautiful windows of Heriot's Hospital,
Tammy bundled his books under the table-tomb
of Mistress Jean Grant, went over to the rear of
the Guildhall at the top of the Row, and threw
a handful of gravel up to Ailie's window. Because of a grandmither Ailie, too, dwelt on a low
level. Her eager little face, lighted by sleep-
dazzled blue eyes, popped out with the surprising
suddenness of the manikins in a Punch-and-Judy
show.

"In juist ane meenit, Tammy," she whispered,
"no' to wauken the grandmither." It was
in so very short a minute that the lassie climbed
out onto the classic pediment of a tomb and
dropped into the kirkyard that her toilet was
uncompleted. Tammy buttoned her washed-
out cotton gown at the back, and she sat on a
slab to lace her shoes. If the fun of giving
Bobby his bath was to be enjoyed to the full

there must be no unnecessary delay. This consideration led Tammy to observe:

"Ye're no' needin' to comb yer hair, Ailie. It leuks bonny eneugh."

In truth, Ailie was one of those fortunate lassies whose crinkly, gold-brown mop really looked best when in some disorder; and of that advantage the little maid was well aware.

"I ken a' that, Tammy. I aye gie it a lick or twa wi' a comb the nicht afore. Ca' the wee doggie."

Bobby fully understood that he was wanted for some serious purpose, but it was a fresh morning of dew and he, apparently, was in the highest of spirits. So he gave Ailie a chase over the sparkling grass and under the showery shrubbery. When he dropped at last on Auld Jock's grave Tammy captured him. The little dog could always be caught there, in a caressable state of exhaustion or meditation, for, sooner or later, he returned to the spot from every bit of work or play. No one would have known it for a place of burial at all. Mr. Brown knew it only by the rose bush at its head and by Bobby's haunting it, for the mound had sunk to the general level of the terrace on which it lay, and spreading crocuses poked their purple and gold noses through the crisp spring turf. But for the wee, guardian dog the man who lay beneath had long lost what little identity he had ever possessed.

Now, as the three lay there, the lassie as flushed and damp as some water-nymph, Bobby panting and submitting to a petting, Tammy took the little dog's muzzle between his thin hands, parted the veil, and looked into the soft brown eyes.

"Leuk, Ailie, Bobby's wantin' somethin', an' is juist haudin' 'imsel'."

It was true. For all his gaiety in play and his energy at work Bobby's eyes had ever a patient, wistful look, not unlike the crippled laddie's. Ah, who can say that it did not require as much courage and gallant bravado on the part of that small, bereft creature to enable him to live at all, as it did for Tammy to face his handicapped life and "no' to remember 'is bad legs"?

In the bath on the rear steps of the lodge Bobby swam and splashed, and scattered foam with his excited tail. He would not stand still to be groomed, but wriggled and twisted and leaped upon the children, putting his shaggy wet paws roguishly in their faces. But he stood there at last, after the jolliest romp, in which the old kirkyard rang with laughter, and oh! so bonny, in his rippling coat of dark silver. No

sooner was he released than he dashed around
the kirk and back again, bringing his latest bone
in his mouth. To his scratching on the stone
sill, for he had been taught not to scratch on the
panel, the door was opened by snod and smiling
Mistress Jeanie, who invited these slum bairns
into such a cozy, spotless kitchen as was not
possible in the tenements. Mr. Brown sat by
the hearth, bundled in blue and white blankets
of wonderfully blocked country weaving. Bobby
put his fore paws on the caretaker's chair and
laid his precious bone in the man's lap.

"Eh, ye takin' bit rascal; loup!" Bobby
jumped to the patted knee, turned around and
around on the soft bed that invited him, licked
the beaming old face to show his sympathy
and friendliness, and jumped down again. Mr.
Brown sighed because Bobby steadily but amiably refused to be anybody's lap-dog. The caretaker turned to the admiring children.

"Ilka morn he fetches 'is bit bane up, thinkin'
it a braw giftie for an ill man. An' syne he
veesits me twa times i' the day, juist bidin' a
wee on the hearthstane, lollin' 'is tongue an'
waggin' 'is tail, cheerfu'-like. Bobby has mair
gude sense in 'is heid than mony a man wha
comes ben the hoose, wi' a lang face, to let me
ken I'm gangin' to dee. Gin I keep snug an'

canny it wullna gang to the heart. Jeanie, woman, fetch ma fife, wull ye?"

Then there were strange doings in the kirkyard lodge. James Brown "wasna gangin' to dee" before his time came, at any rate. In his youth, as under-gardener on a Highland estate, he had learned to play the piccola flute, and lately he had revived the pastoral art of piping just because it went so well with Bobby's delighted legs. To the sonsie air of "Bonnie Dundee" Bobby hopped and stepped and louped, and he turned about on his hind feet, his shagged fore paws drooped on his breast as daintily as the hands in the portraits of early Victorian ladies. The fire burned cheerily in the polished grate, and winked on every shining thing in the room; primroses bloomed in the diamond-paned casement; the skylark fluttered up and sang in its cage; the fife whistled as gaily as a blackbird, and the little dog danced with a comic clumsiness that made them all double up with laughter. The place was so full of brightness, and of kind and merry hearts, that there was room for nothing else. Not one of them dreamed that the shadow of the law was even then over this useful and lovable little dog's head.

A glance at the wag-at-the-wa' clock reminded Ailie that Mr. Traill might be waiting for Bobby.

Curious about the mystery, the children took the little dog down to the gate, happily. They were sobered, however, when Mr. Traill appeared, looking very grand in his Sabbath clothes. He inspected Bobby all over with anxious scrutiny, and gave each of the bairns a threepenny-bit, but he had no blithe greeting for them. Much pre-occupied, he went off at once, with the animated little muff of a dog at his heels. In truth, Mr. Traill was thinking about how he might best plead Bobby's cause with the Lord Provost. The note that was handed him, on leaving the Burgh court the day before, had read:

"Meet me at the Regent's Tomb in St. Giles at eight o'clock in the morning, and bring the wee Highlander with you.—GLENORMISTON."

On the first reading the landlord's spirits had risen, out of all proportion to the cause, owing to his previous depression. But, after all, the appointment had no official character, since the Regent's Tomb in St. Giles had long been a sort of town pump for the retailing of gossip and for the transaction of trifling affairs of all sorts. The fate of this little dog was a small matter, indeed, and so it might be thought fitting, by the powers that be, that it should be decided at the Regent's Tomb rather than in the Burgh court.

To the children, who watched from the kirkyard gate until Mr. Traill and Bobby were hidden
by the buildings on the bridge, it was no' canny.
The busy landlord lived mostly in shirt-sleeves
and big white apron, ready to lend a hand in the
rush hours, and he never was known to put on
his black coat and tall hat on a week-day, except
to attend a funeral. However, there was the
day's work to be done. Tammy had a lesson
still to get, and returned to the kirkyard, and
Ailie ran up to the dining-rooms. On the step
she collided with a red-headed, freckle-faced
young man who asked for Mr. Traill.

'He isna here." The shy lassie was made
almost speechless by recognizing, in this neat,
well-spoken clerk, an old Heriot boy, once as poor
as herself.

"Do you wark for him, lassie? Weel, do you
know how he cam' out in the Burgh court about
the bit dog?"

There was only one "bit dog" in the world to
Ailie. Wild-eyed with alarm at mention of the
Burgh court, in connection with that beloved
little pet, she stammered: "It's—it's—no' a
coort he gaed to. Maister Traill's tak'n Bobby
awa' to a braw kirk."

Sandy nodded his head. "Ay, that would be
the police office in St. Giles. Lassie, tell Mr

Traill I sent the Lord Provost, and if he's needing a witness to ca' on Sandy McGregor."

Ailie stared after him with frightened eyes. Into her mind flashed that ominous remark of the policeman two days before: "I didna ken ye had a dog, John?" She overtook Sandy in front of the sheriff's court on the bridge.

"What—what hae the police to do wi' bittie dogs?"

"If a dog has nae master to pay for his license the police can tak' him up and put him out o' the way."

"Hoo muckle siller are they wantin'?"

"Seven shullings. Gude day, lassie; I'm fair iate." Sandy was not really alarmed about Bobby since the resourceful Mr. Traill had taken up his cause, and he had no idea of the panic of grief and fright that overwhelmed this forlorn child.

Seven shullings! It was an enormous sum to the tenement bairn, whose half-blind grand-mither knitted and knitted in a dimly lighted room, and hoarded halfpennies and farthings to save herself from pauper burial. Seven shullings would pay a month's rent for any one of the crowded rooms in which a family lived. Ailie herself, an untrained lassie who scarcely knew the use of a toasting-fork, was overpaid by generous Mr. Traill at sixpence a day. Seven shullings to permit one little dog to live! It did not occur to Ailie that this was a sum Mr. Traill could easily pay. No' onybody at all had seven shullings all at once! But, oh! everybody had pennies and halfpennies and farthings, and she and Tammy together had a sixpence.

Darting back to the gate, to catch the laddie before he could be off to school, she ran straight into the policeman, who stood with his hand on the wicket. He eyed her sharply.

"Eh, lassie, I was gangin' to spier at the lodge, gin there's a bit dog leevin' i' the kirkyaird."

"I—I—dinna ken." Her voice was unmanageable. She had left to her only the tenement-bred instinct of concealment of any and all facts from an officer of the law.

"Ye dinna ken! Maister Traill said i' the coort a' the bairns aboot kenned the dog. Was he leein'?"

The question stung her into angry admission. "He wadna be leein'. But—but—the bittie——dog—isna here noo."

"Syne, whaur is he? Oot wi' it!"

"I—dinna—ken!" She cowered in abject fear against the wall. She could not know that this officer was suffering a bad attack of shame for his shabby part in the affair. Satisfied that the little dog really did live in the kirkyard, ne turned back to the bridge. When Tammy came out presently he found Ailie crumpled up in a limp little heap in the gateway alcove. In a moment the tale of Bobby's peril was told. The laddie dropped his books and his crutches on the pavement, and his head in his helpless arms, and cried. He had small faith in Ailie's suddenly conceived plan to collect the seven shullings among the dwellers in the tenements.

"Do ye ken hoo muckle siller seven shullin's wad be? It's auchty-fower pennies, a hundred an' saxty-aucht ha'pennies an'—an'—I canna think hoo mony farthings."

"I dinna care a bittie bit. There's mair folk aroond the kirkyaird than there's farthings i' twa, three times seven shullin's. An' maist ilka body kens Bobby. An' we hae a saxpence atween us noo."

"Maister Brown wad gie us anither saxpence gin he had ane," Tammy suggested, wistfully.

"Nae, he's fair ill. Gin he doesna keep canny it wull gang to 'is heart. He'd be aff 'is heid aboot Bobby. Oh, Tammy, Maister Traill gaed to gie 'im up! He was wearin' a' 'is gude claes an' a lang face, to gang to Bobby's buryin'."

This dreadful thought spurred them to instant action. By way of mutual encouragement they

went together through the sculptured doorway
that bore the arms of the ancient guild of the
candlemakers on the lintel, and into the carting
office on the front

"Do ye ken Greyfriars Bobby?" Tammy asked,
timidly, of the man in charge.

He glowered at the laddie and shook his head.
"Havers, mannie; there's no' onybody named
for an auld buryin' groond."

The children fled. There was no use at all in
wasting time on folk who did not know Bobby,
for it would take too long to explain him. But,
alas, they soon discovered that "maist ilka body"
did not know the little dog, as they had so con-
fidently supposed. He was sure to be known
only in the rooms at the rear that overlooked the
kirkyard, and, as one went upward, his identity
became less and less distinct. He was such a
wee, wee, canny terrier, and so many of the
windows had their views constantly shut out by
washings. Around the inner courts, where unkempt women brought every sort of work out to
the light on the galleries and mended worthless
rags, gossiped, and nursed their babies on the
stairs, Bobby had sometimes been heard of, but
almost never seen. Children often knew him
where their elders did not. By the time Ailie
and Tammy had worked swiftly down to the

bottom of the Row other children began to follow them, moved by the peril of the little dog
to sympathy and eager sacrifice.

"Bide a wee, Ailie!" cried one, running to over-
take the lassie. "Here's a penny. I was gangin'
for milk for the porridge. We can do wi'oot the
day."

And there was the money for the broth bone,
and the farthing that would have filled the
gude-man's evening pipe, and the ha'penny for
the grandmither's tea. It was the world-over
story of the poor helping the poor. The progress
of Ailie and Tammy through the tenements was
like that of the piper through Hamelin. The
children gathered and gathered, and followed at
their heels, until a curiously quiet mob of three-
score or more crouched in the court of the old hall
of the Knights of St. John, in the Grassmarket, to
count the many copper coins in Tammy's woolen
bonnet.

"Five shullin's, ninepence, an' a ha'penny,"
Tammy announced. And then, after calculation
on his fingers, "It' ll tak' a shullin' an' twapenny ha'penny mair."

There was a gasping breath of bitter disappointment, and one wee laddie wailed for lost
Bobby. At that Ailie dashed the tears from her
own eyes and sprang up, spurred to desperate

effort. She would storm the all but hopeless attic chambers. Up the twisting turnpike stairs on the outer wall she ran, to where the swallows wheeled about the cornices, and she could hear the iron cross of the Knights Templars creak above the gable. Then, all the way along a dark passage, at one door after another, she knocked, and cried:

"Do ye ken Greyfriars Bobby?"

At some of the doors there was no answer. At others students stared out at the bairn, not in the least comprehending this wild crying. Tears of anger and despair flooded the little maid's blue eyes when she beat on the last door of the row with her doubled fist.

"Do ye ken Greyfriars Bobby? The police are gangin' to mak' 'im be deid—" As the door was flung open she broke into stormy weeping.

"Hey, lassie. I know the dog. What fashes you?"

There stood a tall student, a wet towel about his head, and, behind him, the rafters of the dormer-lighted closet were as thickly hung with bunches of dried herbs from the Botanical Garden as any auld witch-wife's kitchen.

"Oh, are ye kennin' 'im? Isna he bonny an' sonsie? Gie me the shullin' an' twapenny ha'-

penny we're needin', so the police wullna put 'im awa'."

"Losh! It's a license you're wanting? I wish I had as many shullings as I've had gude times with Bobby, and naething to pay for his braw company."

For this was Geordie Ross, going through the Medical College with the help of Heriot's fund that, large as it was, was never quite enough for all the poor and ambitious youths of Edinburgh. And so, although provided for in all necessary ways, his pockets were nearly as empty as of old. He could spare a sixpence if he made his dinner on a potato and a smoked herring. That he was very willing to do, once he had heard the tale, and he went with Ailie to the lodgings of other students, and demanded their siller with no explanation at all.

"Give the lassie what you can spare, man, or I'll have to give you a licking," was his gay and convincing argument, from door to door, until the needed amount was made up. Ailie fled recklessly down the stairs, and cried triumphantly to the upward-looking, silent crowd that had grown and grown around Tammy, like some host of children crusaders.

While Ailie and Tammy were collecting the price of his ransom Bobby was exploring the intricately cut-up interior of old St. Giles, sniffing at the rifts in flimsily plastered partitions that the Lord Provost pointed out to Mr. Traill. Rats were in those crumbling walls. If there had been a hole big enough to admit him, the plucky little dog would have gone in after them. Forbidden to enlarge one, Bobby could only poke his indignant muzzle into apertures, and brace himself as for a fray. And, at the very smell of him, there were such squeakings and scamperings in hidden runways as to be almost beyond a terrier's endurance. The Lord Provost watched him with an approving eye.

"When these partitions are tak'n down Bobby would be vera useful in ridding our noble old cathedral of vermin. But that will not be in this wee Highlander's day nor, I fear, in mine." About the speech of this Peebles man, who had risen from poverty to distinction, learning, wealth, and many varieties of usefulness, there was still an engaging burr. And his manner was so simple that he put the humblest at his ease.

There had been no formality about the meeting at all. Glenormiston was standing in a rear doorway of the cathedral near the Regent's Tomb, looking out into the sunny square of Parliament Close, when Mr. Traill and Bobby appeared. Near seventy, at that time, a back-

ward sweep of white hair and a downward flow
of square-cut, white beard framed a boldly
featured face and left a generous mouth uncovered.

"Gude morning, Mr. Traill. So that is the
famous dog that has stood sentinel for more than
eight years. He should be tak'n up to the Castle
and shown to young soldiers who grumble at
twenty-four hours' guard duty. How do you do,
sir!" The great man, whom the Queen knighted
later, and whom the University he was too
poor to attend as a lad honored with a degree,
stooped from the Regent's Tomb and shook
Bobby's lifted paw with grave courtesy. Then,
leaving the little dog to entertain himself, he
turned easily to his own most absorbing interest
of the moment.

"Do you happen to care for Edinburgh antiquities, Mr. Traill? Reformation piety made
sad havoc of art everywhere. Man, come here!"

Down into the lime dust the Lord Provost and
the landlord went, in their good black clothes,
for a glimpse of a bit of sculpturing on a tomb
that had been walled in to make a passage. A
loose brick removed, behind and above it, the
sun flashed through fragments of emerald and
ruby glass of a saint's robe, in a bricked-up
window. Such buried and forgotten treasure,

Glenormiston explained, filled the entire south transept. In the High Kirk, that then filled the eastern end of the cathedral, they went up a cheap wooden stairway, to the pew-filled gallery that was built into the old choir, and sat down. Mr. Traill's eyes sparkled. Glenormiston was a man after his own heart, and they were getting along famously; but, oh! it began to seem more and more unlikely that a Lord Provost, who was concerned about such braw things as the restoration of the old cathedral and letting the sun into the ancient tenements, should be much interested in a small, masterless dog.

"Man, auld John Knox will turn over in his bit grave in Parliament Close if you put a 'kist o' whustles' in St. Giles." Mr. Traill laughed.

"I admit I might have stopped short of the organ but for the courageous example of Doctor Lee in Greyfriars. It was from him that I had a quite extravagant account of this wee, leal Highlander a few years ago. I have aye meant to go to see him, but I'm a busy man and the matter passed out of mind. Mr. Traill, I'm your sadly needed witness. I heard you from the doorway of the court-room, and I sent up a note confirming your story and asking, as a courtesy, that the case be turned over to me for some exceptional disposal. Would you mind telling another man the tale that so moved Doctor Lee? I've aye had a fondness for the human document."

So there, above the pulpit of the High Kirk of St. Giles, the tale was told again, so strangely did this little dog's life come to be linked with the highest and lowest, the proudest and humblest in the Scottish capital. Now, at mention of Auld Jock, Bobby put his shagged paws up inquiringly on the edge of the pew, so that Mr. Traill lifted him. He lay down flat between the two men, with his nose on his paws, and his little tousled head under the Lord Provost's hand.

Auld Jock lived again in that recital. Glenormiston, coming from the country of the Ettrick shepherd, knew such lonely figures, and the pathos of old age and waning powers that drove them in to the poor quarters of towns. There was pictured the stormy night and the simple old man who sought food and shelter, with the devoted little dog that "wasna 'is ain." Sick unto death he was, and full of ignorant prejudices and fears that needed wise handling. And there was the well-meaning landlord's blunder, humbly confessed, and the obscure and tragic result of it, in a foul and swarming rookery "juist aff the Coogate."

"Man, it was Bobby that told me of his master's condition. He begged me to help Auld Jock, and what did I do but let my fule tongue wag about doctors. I nae more than turned my back than the auld body was awa' to his meeserable death. It has aye eased my conscience a bit to feed the dog."

"That's not the only reason why you have fed him." There was a twinkle in the Lord Provost's eye, and Mr. Traill blushed.

"Weel, I'll admit to you that I'm fair fulish about Bobby. Man, I've courted that sma' terrier for eight and a half years. He's as polite and friendly as the deil, but he'll have naething to do with me or with onybody. I wonder the intelligent bit doesn't bite me for the ill turn I did his master."

Then there was the story of Bobby's devotion to Auld Jock's memory to be told—the days when he faced starvation rather than desert that grave, the days when he lay cramped under the fallen table-tomb, and his repeated, dramatic escapes from the Pentland farm. His never-broken silence in the kirkyard was only to be explained by the unforgotten orders of his dead master. His intelligent effort to make himself useful to the caretaker had won indulgence. His ready obedience, good temper, high spirits and friendliness had made him the special pet of the tenement children and the Heriot laddies. At the very last Mr. Traill repeated the talk he had had with the non-commissioned officer from the Castle, and confessed his own fear of some forlorn end for Bobby. It was true he was nobody's dog; and he was fascinated by soldiers and military music, and so, perhaps—

"I'll no' be reconciled to parting— Eh, man, that's what Auld Jock himsel' said when he was telling me that the bit dog must be returned to the sheep-farm: 'It wull be sair partin'.'" Tears stood in the unashamed landlord's eyes.

Glenormiston was pulling Bobby's silkily fringed ears thoughtfully. Through all this talk about his dead master the little dog had not stirred. For the second time that day Bobby's veil was pushed back, first by the most unfortunate laddie in the decaying tenements about Greyfriars, and now by the Lord Provost of the ancient royal burgh and capital of Scotland. And both made the same discovery. Deep-brown pools of love, young Bobby's eyes had dwelt upon Auld Jock. Pools of sad memories they were now, looking out wistfully and patiently upon a masterless world.

"Are you thinking he would be reconciled to be anywhere away from that grave? Look, man!"

"Lord forgive me! I aye thought the wee doggie happy enough."

After a moment the two men went down the gallery stairs in silence. Bobby dropped from the bench and fell into a subdued trot at their heels. As they left the cathedral by the door that led into High Street Glenormiston remarked, with a mysterious smile:

"I'm thinking Edinburgh can do better by wee Bobby than to banish him to the Castle. But wait a bit, man. A kirk is not the place for settling a small dog's affairs."

The Lord Provost led the way westward along the cathedral's front. On High Street, St. Giles had three doorways. The middle door then gave admittance to the police office; the western opened into the Little Kirk, popularly known as Haddo's Hole. It was into this bare, white-washed chapel that Glenormiston turned to get some restoration drawings he had left on the pulpit. He was explaining them to Mr. Traill when he was interrupted by a murmur and a shuffle, as of many voices and feet, and an odd tap-tap-tapping in the vestibule.

Of all the doorways on the north and south fronts of St. Giles the one to the Little Kirk was nearest the end of George IV. Bridge. Confused by the vast size and imposing architecture of the old cathedral, these slum children, in search of the police office, went no farther, but ventured timidly into the open vestibule of Haddo's Hole. Any doubts they might have had about this being the right place were soon dispelled. Bobby heard them and darted out to investigate. And suddenly they were all inside, overwrought Ailie on the floor, clasping the little dog and crying hysterically:

"Bobby's no' deid! Bobby's no' deid! Oh, Maister Traill, ye wullna hae to gie 'im up to the police! Tammy's got the seven shullin's in 'is bonnet!"

And there was small Tammy, crutches dropped and pouring that offering of love and mercy out at the foot of an altar in old St. Giles. Such an astonishing pile of copper coins it was, that it looked to the landlord like the loot of some shop-keeper's change drawer.

"Eh, puir laddie, whaur did ye get it a' noo?" he asked, gravely.

Tammy was very self-possessed and proud. "The bairnies aroond the kirkyaird gie'd it to pay the police no' to mak' Bobby be deid."

Mr. Traill flashed a glance at Glenormiston. It was a look at once of triumph and of humility over the Herculean deed of these disinherited children. But the Lord Provost was gazing at that crowd of pale bairns, products of the Old Town's ancient slums, and feeling, in his own person, the civic shame of it. And he was thinking, thinking, that he must hasten that other project nearest his heart, of knocking holes in solid rows of foul cliffs, in the Cowgate, on High Street, and around Greyfriars. It was an incredible thing that such a flower of affection should have bloomed so sweetly in such sunless cells. And it was a new gospel, at that time, that a dog or a horse or a bird might have its mission in this world of making people kinder and happier.

They were all down on the floor, in the space before the altar, unwashed, uncombed, unconscious of the dirty rags that scarce covered them; quite happy and self-forgetful in the charming friskings and friendly lollings of the well-fed, carefully groomed, beautiful little dog. Ailie, still so excited that she forgot to be shy, put Bobby through his pretty tricks. He rolled over and over, he jumped, he danced to Tammy's whistling of "Bonnie Dundee," he walked on his hind legs and louped at a bonnet, he begged, he lifted his short shagged paw and shook hands. Then he sniffed at the heap of coins, looked up inquiringly at Mr. Traill, and, concluding that here was some property to be guarded, stood by

GREYFRIARS BOBBY

the "siller" as stanchly as a soldier. It was just
pure pleasure to watch him.

Very suddenly the Lord Provost changed his
mind. A sacred kirk was the very best place of
all to settle this little dog's affairs. The offering
of these children could not be refused. It should
lie there, below the altar, and be consecrated to
some other blessed work; and he would do now
and here what he had meant to do elsewhere and
in a quite different way. He lifted Bobby to the
pulpit so that all might see him, and he spoke
so that all might understand.

"Are ye kennin' what it is to gie the freedom
o' the toon to grand folk?"

"It's—it's when the bonny Queen comes an'
ye gie her the keys to the burgh gates that are
no' here ony mair." Tammy, being in Heriot's,
was a laddie of learning.

"Weel done, laddie. Lang syne there was a
wa' aroond Edinburgh wi' gates in it." Oh yes,
all these bairnies knew that, and the fragment of
it that was still to be seen outside and above the
Grassmarket, with its sentry tower by the old west
port. "Gin a fey king or ither grand veesitor
cam', the Laird Provost an' the maigestrates gied
'im the keys so he could gang in an' oot at 'is
pleesure. The wa's are a' doon noo, an' the
gates no' here ony mair, but we hae the keys, an'

we mak' a show o' gien' 'em to veesitors wha are
vera grand or wise or gude, or juist usefu' by the
ordinar'."

"Maister Gladstane," said Tammy.

"Ay, we honor the Queen's meenisters; an'
Miss Nightingale, wha nursed the soldiers i'
the war; an' Leddy Burdett-Coutts, wha gies a'
her siller an' a' her heart to puir folk an' is aye
kind to horses and dogs an' singin' birdies; an'
we gie the keys to heroes o' the war wha are
brave an' faithfu'. An' noo, there's a wee bit
beastie. He's weel-behavin', an' isna makin' a
blatterin' i' an auld kirkyaird. He aye minds
what he's bidden to do. He's cheerfu' an' busy,
keepin' the proolin' pussies an' vermin frae the
sma' birdies i' the nests. He mak's friends o'
ilka body, an' he's faithfu'. For a deid man he
lo'ed he's gaun hungry; an' he hasna forgotten 'im
or left 'im by 'is lane at nicht for mair years than
some o' ye are auld. An' gin ye find 'im lyin'
canny, an' ye tak' a keek into 'is bonny brown
een, ye can see he's aye greetin'. An' so, ye
didna ken why, but ye a' lo'ed the lanely wee—"

"Bobby!" It was an excited breath of a word
from the wide-eyed bairns.

"Bobby! Havers! A bittie dog wadna ken
what to do wi' keys."

But Glenormiston was smiling, and these sharp-

witted slum bairns exchanged knowing glances.
"Whaur's that sma'—?" He dived into this
pocket and that, making a great pretense of
searching, until he found a narrow band of new
leather, with holes in one end and a stout buckle
on the other, and riveted fast in the middle of it
was a shining brass plate. Tammy read the inscription aloud:

GREYFRIARS BOBBY

FROM THE LORD PROVOST

1867   Licensed

The wonderful collar was passed from hand to
hand in awed silence. The children stared and
stared at this white-haired and bearded man,
who "wasna grand ava," but who talked to them
as simply and kindly as a grandfaither. He
went right on talking to them in his homely way
to put them at their ease, telling them that nobody at all, not even the bonny Queen, could be
more than kind and well-behaving and faithful
to duty. Wee Bobby was all that, and so:
"Gin dizzens an' dizzens o' bairns war kennin'
'im, an' wad fetch seven shullin's i' their ha'-
pennies to a kirk, they could buy the richt for
the braw doggie to be leevin', the care o' them a',

i' the auld kirkyaird o' Greyfriars. An' he maun hae the collar so the police wull ken 'im an' no' ever tak' 'im up for a puir, gaen-aboot dog."

The children quite understood the responsibility they assumed, and their eyes shone with pride at the feeling that, if more fortunate friends failed, this little creature must never be allowed to go hungry. And when he came to die—oh, in a very, very few years, for they must remember that "a doggie isna as lang-leevin' as folk"—they must not forget that Bobby would not be permitted to be buried in the kirkyard.

"We'll gie 'im a grand buryin'," said Tammy. "We'll find a green brae by a babblin' burn aneath a snawy hawthorn, whaur the throstle sings an' the blackbird whustles." For the crippled laddie had never forgotten Mr. Traill's description of a proper picnic, and that must, indeed, be a wee dog's heaven.

"Ay, that wull do fair weel." The collar had come back to him by this time, and the Lord Provost buckled it securely about Bobby's neck.

X

THE music of bagpipe, fife and drum brought them all out of Haddo's Hole into High Street. It was the hour of the morning drill, and the soldiers were marching out of the Castle. From the front of St. Giles, that jutted into the steep thoroughfare, they could look up to where the street widened to the esplanade on Castle Hill. Rank after rank of scarlet coats, swinging kilts and sporrans, and plumed bonnets appeared. The sun flashed back from rifle barrels and bayonets and from countless bright buttons.

A number of the older laddies ran up the climbing street. Mr. Traill called Bobby back and, with a last grip of Glenormiston's hand, set off across the bridge. To the landlord the world seemed a brave place to be living in, the fabric of earth and sky and human society to be woven of kindness. Having urgent business of buying supplies in the markets at Broughton and Lauriston, Mr. Traill put Bobby inside the kirk-yard gate and hurried away to get into his every-day clothing. After dinner, or tea, he promised

himself the pleasure of an hour at the lodge, **to**
tell Mr. Brown the wonderful news, and to show
him Bobby's braw collar.

When, finally, he was left alone, Bobby trotted
around the kirk, to assure himself that Auld
Jock's grave was unmolested.   There he turned
on his back, squirmed and rocked on the crocuses,
and tugged at the unaccustomed collar.   His
inverted struggles, low growlings and furry con-
tortions set the wrens to scolding and the redbreasts to making nervous inquiries.   Much nest-
building, tuneful courtship, and masculine blus-
tering was going on, and there was little police
duty for Bobby.   After a time he sat up on the
table-tomb, pensively.   With Mr. Brown con-
fined to the lodge, and Mistress Jeanie in close
attendance upon him there, the kirkyard was a
lonely place for a sociable little dog; and a soft,
spring day given over to brooding beside a
beloved grave, was quite too heart-breaking a
thing to contemplate.   Just for cheerful occupation Bobby had another tussle with the collar.
He pulled it so far under his thatch that no one
could have guessed that he had a collar on at all,
when he suddenly righted himself and scampered
away to the gate.

The music grew louder and came nearer.   The
first of the route-marching that the Castle garri-

son practised on occasional, bright spring mornings was always a delightful surprise to the small
boys and dogs of Edinburgh. Usually the soldiers went down High Street and out to Porto-
bello on the sea. But a regiment of tough and
wiry Highlanders often took, by preference, the
mounting road to the Pentlands to get a whiff of
heather in their nostrils.

On they came, band playing, colors flying,
feet moving in unison with a march, across the
viaduct bridge into Greyfriars Place. Bobby
was up on the wicket, his small, energetic body
quivering with excitement from his muzzle to
his tail. If Mr. Traill had been there he would
surely have caught the infection, thrown care to
this sweet April breeze for once, and taken the
wee terrier for a run on the Pentland braes. The
temptation was going by when a preoccupied
lady, with a sheaf of Easter lilies on her sable
arm, opened the wicket. Her ample Victorian
skirts swept right over the little dog, and when
he emerged there was the gate slightly ajar.
Widening the aperture with nose and paws,
Bobby was off, skirmishing at large on the rear
and flanks of the troops, down the Burghmuir.

It may never have happened, in the years since
Auld Jock died and the farmer of Cauldbrae gave
up trying to keep him on the hills, that Bobby

had gone so far back on this once familiar road; and he may not have recognized it at first, for the highways around Edinburgh were everywhere much alike. This one alone began to climb again. Up, up it toiled, for two weary miles, to the hilltop toll-bar of Fairmilehead, and there the sounds and smells that made it different from other roads began.

Five miles out of the city the halt was called, and the soldiers flung themselves on the slope. Many experiences of route-marching had taught Bobby that there was an interval of rest before the return, so, with his nose to the ground, he started up the brae on a pilgrimage to old shrines. Just as in his puppyhood days, at Auld Jock's heels, there was much shouting of men, barking of collies, and bleating of sheep all the way up. Once he had to leave the road until a driven flock had passed. Behind the sheep walked an old laborer in hodden-gray, woolen bonnet, and shepherd's twa-fold plaid, with a lamb in the pouch of it. Bobby trembled at the apparition, sniffed at the hob-nailed boots, and then, with drooped head and tail, trotted on up the slope.

Men and dogs were all out on the billowy pastures, and the farm-house of Cauldbrae lay on the level terrace, seemingly deserted and steeped

in memories. A few moments before, a tall lassie
had come out to listen to the military music.
A couple of hundred feet below, the coats of the
soldiers looked to her like poppies scattered on
the heather. At the top of the brae the wind
was blowing a cold gale, so the maidie went up
again, and around to a bit of tangled garden on
the sheltered side of the house. The "wee
lassie Elsie" was still a bairn in short skirts
and braids, who lavished her soft heart, as yet,
on briar bushes and daisies.

Bobby made a tour of the sheepfold, the cow-
yard and byre, and he lingered behind the byre,
where Auld Jock had played with him on Sabbath afternoons. He inspected the dairy, and
the poultry-house where hens were sitting on
their nests. By and by he trotted around the
house and came upon the lassie, busily clearing
winter rubbish from her posie bed. A dog
changes very little in appearance, but in eight
and a half years a child grows into a different
person altogether. Bobby barked politely to
let this strange lassie know that he was there.
In the next instant he knew her, for she whirled
about and, in a kind of glad wonder, cried
out:

"Oh, Bobby! hae ye come hame? Mither,
here's ma ain wee Bobby!" For she had never

given up the hope that this adored little pet
would some day return to her.

"Havers, lassie, ye're aye seein' Bobby i' ilka
Hielan' terrier, an' there's mony o' them aboot."

The gude-wife looked from an attic window in
the steep gable, and then hurried down. "Weel,
noo, ye're richt, Elsie. He wad be comin' wi'
the regiment frae the Castle. Bittie doggies an'
laddies are fair daft aboot the soldiers. Ay, he's
bonny, an' weel cared for, by the ordinar'. I
wonder gin he's still leevin' i' the grand auld
kirkyaird."

Wary of her remembered endearments, Bobby
kept a safe distance from the maidie, but he sat
up and lolled his tongue, quite willing to pay
her a friendly visit. From that she came to a
wrong conclusion: "Sin' he cam' o' his ain
accord he's like to bide." Her eyes were blue
stars.

"I wadna be coontin' on that, lassie. An' I
wadna sneck a door on 'im anither time. Gin
he wanted to get oot he'd dig aneath a floor o'
stane. Leuk at that, noo! The bonny wee is
greetin' for Auld Jock."

It was true, for, on entering the kitchen, Bobby
went straight to the bench in the corner and lay
down flat under it. Elsie sat beside him, just as
she had done of old. Her eyes overflowed so in

sympathy that the mother was quite distract
This would not do at all.

"Lassie, are ye no' rememberin' Bobby was
fair fond o' moor-hens' eggs fried wi' bits o'
cheese? He wullna be gettin' thae things; an' it
wad be maist michty, noo, gin ye couldna win
the bittie dog awa' frae the reekie auld toon.
Gang oot wi' 'im an' rin on the brae an' bid 'im
find the nests aneath the whins."

In a moment they were out on the heather, and
it seemed, indeed, as if Bobby might be won.
He frisked and barked at Elsie's heels, chased
rabbits and flushed the grouse; and when he ran
into a peat-darkened tarn, rimmed with moss,
he had such a cold and splashy swim as quite to
give a little dog a distaste for warm, soapy water
in a claes tub. He shook and ran himself dry,
and he raced the laughing child until they both
dropped panting on the wind-rippled heath.
Then he hunted on the ground under the gorse
for those nests that had a dozen or more eggs
in them. He took just one from each in his
mouth, as Auld Jock had taught him to do. On
the kitchen hearth he ate the savory meal with
much satisfaction and polite waggings. But
when the bugle sounded from below to form
ranks, he pricked his drop ears and started for
the door.

Before he knew what had happened he was inside the poultry-house. In another instant he was digging frantically in the soft earth under the door. When the lassie lay down across the crack he stopped digging, in consternation. His sense of smell told him what it was that shut out the strip of light; and a bairn's soft body is not a proper object of attack for a little dog, no matter how desperate the emergency. There was no time to be lost, for the drums began to beat the march. Having to get out very quickly, Bobby did a forbidden thing: swiftly and noisily he dashed around the dark place, and there arose such wild squawkings and rushings of wings as to bring the gude-wife out of the house in alarm.

"Lassie, I canna hae the bittie dog in wi' the broodin' chuckies!"

She flung the door wide. Bobby shot through, and into Elsie's outstretched arms. She held to him desperately, while he twisted and struggled and strained away; and presently something shining worked into view, through the disordered thatch about his neck. The mother had come to the help of the child, and it was she who read the inscription on the brazen plate aloud.

"Preserve us a'! Lassie, he's been tak'n by the Laird Provost an' gien the name o' the auld

kirkyaird. He's an ower grand doggie. Ma puir
bairnie, dinna greet so sair!" For the little girl
suddenly released the wee Highlander and sobbed
on her mother's shoulder.

"He isna ma ain Bobby ony mair!" She
"couldna thole" to watch him as he tumbled
down the brae.

On the outward march, among the many dogs
and laddies that had followed the soldiers, Bobby
escaped notice. But most of these had gone
adventuring in Swanston Dell, to return to the
city by the gorge of Leith Water. Now, traveling
three miles to the soldiers' one, scampering in
wide circles over the fields, swimming burns,
scrambling under hedges, chasing whaups into
piping cries, barking and louping in pure exuberance of spirits, many eyes looked upon him
admiringly, and discontented mouths turned upward at the corners. It is not the least of a
little dog's missions in life to communicate his
own irresponsible gaiety to men.

If the return had been over George IV. Bridge
Bobby would, no doubt, have dropped behind
at Mr. Traill's or at the kirkyard. But on the
Burghmuir the troops swung eastward until they
rounded Arthur's Seat and met the cavalry
drilling before the barracks at Piershill. Such
pretty manœuvering of horse and foot took place

below Holyrood Palace as quite to enrapture a
terrier. When the infantry marched up the
Canongate and High Street, the mounted men
following and the bands playing at full blast, the
ancient thoroughfare was quickly lined with
cheering crowds, and faces looked down from
ten tiers of windows on a beautiful spectacle.
Bobby did not know when the bridge-approach
was passed; and then, on Castle Hill, he was in
an unknown region. There the street widened to
the great square of the esplanade. The cavalry
wheeled and dashed down High Street, but the
infantry marched on and up, over the sounding
drawbridge that spanned a dry moat of the
Middle Ages, and through a deep-arched gateway
of masonry.

The outer gate to the Castle was wider than
the opening into many an Edinburgh wynd; but
Bobby stopped, uncertain as to where this
narrow roadway, that curved upward to the
right, might lead. It was not a dark fissure in
a cliff of houses, but was bounded on the outer
side by a loopholed wall, and on the inner by a
rocky ledge of ascending levels. Wherever the
shelf was of sufficient breadth a battery of cannon
was mounted, and such a flood of light fell from
above and flashed on polished steel and brass as
to make the little dog blink in bewilderment.

And he whirled like a rotary sweeper in the dusty road and yelped when the time-gun, in the half-moon battery at the left of the gate and behind him, crashed and shook the massive rock.

He barked and barked, and dashed toward the insulting clamor. The dauntless little dog and his spirited protest were so out of proportion to the huge offense that the guard laughed, and other soldiers ran out of the guard-houses that flanked the gate. They would have put the noisy terrier out at once, but Bobby was off, up the curving roadway into the Castle. The music had ceased, and the soldiers had disappeared over the rise. Through other dark arches of masonry he ran. On the crest were two ways to choose—the roadway on around and past the barracks, and a flight of steps cut steeply in the living rock of the ledge, and leading up to the King's Bastion. Bobby took the stairs at a few bounds.

On the summit there was nothing at all beside a tiny, ancient stone chapel with a Norman arched and sculptured doorway, and guarding it an enormous burst cannon. But these ruins were the crown jewels of the fortifications—their origins lost in legends—and so they were cared for with peculiar reverence. Sergeant Scott of the Royal Engineers himself, in fatigue-dress, was down on his knees before St. Margaret's oratory, pulling from a crevice in the foundations a knot of grass that was at its insidious work of time and change. As Bobby dashed up to the citadel, still barking, the man jumped to his feet. Then he slapped his thigh and laughed. Catching the animated little bundle of protest the sergeant set him up for inspection on the shattered breeching of Mons Meg.

"Losh! The sma' dog cam' by 'is ainsel'! He could no' resist the braw soldier laddies. 'He's a dog o' discreemination,' eh? Gin he bides a wee, noo, it wull tak' the conceit oot o' the innkeeper."

He turned to gather up his tools, for the first dinner bugle was blowing. Bobby knew by the gun that it was the dinner-hour, but he had been fed at the farm and was not hungry. He might as well see a bit more of life. He sat upon the cannon, not in the least impressed by the honor, and lolled his tongue.

In Edinburgh Castle there was nothing to alarm a little dog. A dozen or more large buildings, in three or four groups, and representing many periods of architecture, lay to the south and west on the lowest terraces, and about them were generous parked spaces. Into the largest of the buildings, a long, four-storied barracks, the soldiers had vanished. And now, at the

blowing of a second bugle, half a hundred order-
lies hurried down from a modern cook-house,
near the summit, with cans of soup and meat
and potatoes. The sergeant followed one of
these into a room on the front of the barracks.
In their serge fatigue-tunics the sixteen men
about the long table looked as different from the
gay soldiers of the march as though so many
scarlet and gold and bonneted butterflies had
turned back into sad-colored grubs.

"Private McLean," he called to his batman
who, for one-and-six a week, cared for his be-
longings, "tak' chairge o' the dog, wull ye, an'
fetch 'im to the non-com mess when ye come to
put ma kit i' gude order."

Before he could answer the bombardment of
questions about Bobby the door was opened
again. The men dropped their knives and forks
and stood at attention. The officer of the day
was making the rounds of the forty or fifty such
rooms in the barracks to inquire of the soldiers if
their dinner was satisfactory. He recognized at
once the attractive little Skye that had taken
the eyes of the men on the march, and asked
about him. Sergeant Scott explained that
Bobby had no owner. He was living, by permission, in Greyfriars kirkyard, guarding the
grave of a long-dead, humble master, and was

fed by the landlord of the dining-rooms near the gate. If the little dog took a fancy to garrison life, and the regiment to him, he thought Mr. Traill, who had the best claim upon him, might consent to his transfer to the Castle. After orders, at sunset, he would take Bobby down to the restaurant himself.

"I wish you good luck, Sergeant." The officer whistled, and Bobby leaped upon him and off again, and indulged in many inconsequent friskings. "Before you take him home fetch him over to the officers' mess at dinner. It is guest night, and he is sure to interest the gentlemen. A loyal little creature who has guarded his dead master's grave for more than eight years deserves to have a toast drunk to him by the officers of the Queen. But it's an extraordinary story, and it doesn't sound altogether probable. Jolly little beggar!" He patted Bobby cordially on the side, and went out.

The news of his advent and fragments of his story spread so quickly through the barracks that mess after mess swarmed down from the upper floors and out into the roadway to see Bobby. Private McLean stood in the door, smoking a cutty pipe, and grinning with pride in the merry little ruffian of a terrier, who met the friendly advances of the soldiers more than

half-way. Bobby's guardian would have liked
very well to have sat before the canteen in the
sun and gossiped about his small charge. However, in the sergeant's sleeping-quarters above the
mess-room, he had the little dog all to himself,
and Bobby had the liveliest interest in the boxes
and pots, brushes and sponges, and in the proc-
esses of polishing, burnishing, and pipe-claying
a soldier's boots and buttons and belts. As he
worked at his valeting, the man kept time with
his foot to rude ballads that he sang in such a
hissing Celtic that Bobby barked, scandalized by
a dialect that had been music in the ears of his
ancestors. At that Private McLean danced a
Highland fling for him, and wee Bobby came near
bursting with excitement. When the sergeant
came up to make a magnificent toilet for tea and
for the evening in town, the soldier expressed himself with enthusiasm.

"He iss a deffle of a dog, sir!"

He was thought to be a "deffle of a dog" in
the mess, where the non-com officers had tea at
small writing and card tables. They talked
and laughed very fast and loud, tried Bobby out
on all the pretty tricks he knew, and taught him
to speak and to jump for a lump of sugar balanced
on his nose. They did not fondle him, and this
rough, masculine style of pampering and petting

was very much to his liking. It was a proud thing, too, for a little dog, to walk out with the sergeant's shining boots and twirled walking-stick, and be introduced into one strange place after another all around the Castle.

From tea to tattoo was playtime for the garrison. Many smartly dressed soldiers, with passes earned by good behavior, went out to find amusement in the city. Visitors, some of them tourists from America, made the rounds under the guidance of old soldiers. The sergeant followed such a group of sight-seers through a postern behind the armory and out onto the cliff. There he lounged under a fir-tree above St. Margaret's Well and smoked a dandified cigar, while Bobby explored the promenade and scraped acquaintance with the strangers.

On the northern and southern sides the Castle wall rose from the very edge of sheer precipices. Except for loopholes there were no openings. But on the west there was a grassy terrace without the wall, and below that the cliff fell away a little less steeply. The declivity was clothed sparsely with hazel shrubs, thorns, whins and thistles; and now and then a stunted fir or rowan tree or a group of white-stemmed birks was stoutly rooted on a shelving ledge. Had any one, the visitors asked, ever escaped down this wild crag?

GREYFRIARS BOBBY

Yes, Queen Margaret's children, the guide answered. Their father dead in battle, their saintly mother dead in the sanctuary of her tiny chapel, the enemy battering at the gate, soldiers had lowered the royal lady's body in a basket, and got the orphaned children down, in safety and away, in a fog, over Queen's Ferry to Dunfirmline in the Kingdom of Fife. It was true that a false step or a slip of the foot would have dashed them to pieces on the rocks below. A gentleman of the party scouted the legend. Only a fox or an Alpine chamois could make that perilous descent.

With his head cocked alertly, Bobby had stood listening. Hearing this vague talk of going down, he may have thought these people meant to go, for he quietly dropped over the edge and went, head over heels, ten feet down, and landed in a clump of hazel. A lady screamed. Bobby righted himself and barked cheerful reassurance. The sergeant sprang to his feet and ordered him to come back.

Now, the sergeant was pleasant company, to be sure; but he was not a person who had to be obeyed, so Bobby barked again, wagged his crested tail, and dropped lower. The people who shuddered on the brink could see that the little dog was going cautiously enough; and

presently he looked doubtfully over a sheer fall
of twenty feet, turned and scrambled back to
the promenade. He was cried and exclaimed
over by the hysterical ladies, and scolded for a
bittie fule by the sergeant. To this Bobby returned ostentatious yawns of boredom and non-
chalant lollings, for it seemed a small matter to
be so fashed about. At that a gentleman remarked, testily, to hide his own agitation, that
dogs really had very little sense. The sergeant
ordered Bobby to precede him through the postern, and the little dog complied amiably.

All the afternoon bugles had been blowing.
For each signal there was a different note, and at
each uniformed men appeared and hurried to
new points. Now, near sunset, there was the
fanfare for officers' orders for the next day.
The sergeant put Bobby into Queen Margaret's
Chapel, bade him remain there, and went down
to the Palace Yard. The chapel on the summit
was a convenient place for picking the little dog
up on his way to the officers' mess. Then he
meant to have his own supper cozily at Mr.
Traill's and to negotiate for Bobby.

A dozen people would have crowded this
ancient oratory, but, small as it was, it was fitted
with a chancel-rail and a font for baptizing the
babies born in the Castle. Through the window

above the altar, where the sainted Queen was pictured in stained glass, the sunlight streamed and laid another jeweled image on the stone floor. Then the colors faded, until the holy place became an austere cell. The sun had dropped behind the western Highlands.

Bobby thought it quite time to go home. By day he often went far afield, seeking distraction, but at sunset he yearned for the grave in Grey-friars. The steps up which he had come lay in plain view from the doorway of the chapel. Bobby dropped down the stairs, and turned into the main roadway of the Castle. At the first arch that spanned it a red-coated guard paced on the other side of a closed gate. It would not be locked until tattoo, at nine-thirty, but, without a pass, no one could go in or out. Bobby sprang on the bars and barked, as much as to say: "Come awa', man, I hae to get oot."

The guard stopped, presented arms to this small, peremptory terrier, and inquired face-tiously if he had a pass. Bobby bristled and yelped indignantly. The soldier grinned with amusement. Sentinel duty was lonesome busi-ness, and any diversion a relief. In a guard-house asleep when Bobby came into the Castle, he had not seen the little dog before and knew nothing about him. He might be the property

ɒt one of the regiment ladies. Without orders
he dared not let Bobby out. A furious and futile
onslaught on the gate he met with a jocose feint
of his bayonet. Tiring of the play, presently, the
soldier turned his back and paced to the end of
his beat.

Bobby stopped barking in sheer astonishment.
He gazed after the stiff, retreating back, in
frightened disbelief that he was not to be let out.
He attacked the stone under the barrier, but
quickly discovered its unyielding nature. Then
he howled until the sentinel came back, but when
the man went by without looking at him he
uttered a whimpering cry and fled upward. The
roadway was dark and the dusk was gathering
on the citadel when Bobby dashed across the
summit and down into the brightly lighted
square of the Palace Yard.

The gas-lamps were being lighted on the
bridge, and Mr. Traill was getting into his street-
coat for his call on Mr. Brown when Tammy put
his head in at the door of the restaurant. The
crippled laddie had a warm, uplifted look, for
Love had touched the sordid things of life, and
a miracle had bloomed for the tenement dwellers
around Greyfriars.

"Maister Traill, Mrs. Brown says wull ye
please send Bobby hame. Her gude - mon's

frettin' for 'im; an' syne, a' the folk aroond the kirkyaird hae come to the gate to see the bittie dog's braw collar. They wullna believe the Laird Provost gied it tc 'im for a chairm gin they dinna see it wi' their ain een."

"Why, mannie, Bobby's no' here. He must be in the kirkyard."

"Nae, he isna. I ca'ed, an' Ailie keeked in ilka place amang the stanes."

They stared at each other, the landlord serious, the laddie's lip trembling. Mr. Traill had not returned from his numerous errands about the city until the middle of the afternoon. He thought, of course, that Bobby had been in for his dinner, as usual, and had returned to the kirkyard. It appeared, now, that no one about the dining-rooms had seen the little dog. Everybody had thought that Mr. Traill had taken Bobby with him. He hurried down to the gate to find Mistress Jeanie at the wicket, and a crowd of tene-ment women and children in the alcove and massed down Candlemakers Row. Alarm spread like a contagion. In eight years and more Bobby had not been outside the kirkyard gate after the sunset bugle. Mrs. Brown turned pale.

"Dinna say the bittie dog's lost, Maister Traill. It wad gang to the heart o' ma gude-mon."

"Havers, woman, he's no' lost." Mr. Traill spoke stoutly enough. "Just go up to the lodge and tell Mr. Brown I'm—weel, I'll just attend to that sma' matter my ainsel'." With that he took a gay face and a set-up air into the lodge to meet Mr. Brown's glowering eye.

"Whaur's the dog, man? I've been deaved aboot 'im a' the day, but I haena seen the sonsie rascal nor the braw collar the Laird Provost gied 'im. An' syne, wi' the folk comin' to spier for 'im an' swarmin' ower the kirkyaird, ye'd think a warlock was aboot. Bobby isna your dog—"

"Haud yoursel', man. Bobby's a famous dog. with the freedom of Edinburgh given to him, and naething will do but Glenormiston must show him to a company o' grand folk at his bit country place. He's sending in a cart by a groom, and I'm to tak' Bobby out and fetch him hame after a braw dinner on gowd plate. The bairns meant weel, but they could no' give Bobby a washing fit for a veesit with the nobeelity. I had to tak' him to a barber for a shampoo."

Mr. Brown roared with laughter. "Man, ye hae mair fule notions i' yer heid. Ye'll hae to pay a shullin' or twa to a barber, an' Bobby'll be sae set up there'll be nae leevin' wi' 'im. Sit ye doon an' tell me aboot the collar, man."

"I can no' stop now to wag my tongue.

Here's the gude-wife. I'll just help her get you awa' to your bed."

It was dark when he returned to the gate, and the Castle wore its luminous crown. The lights from the street lamps flickered on the up-turned, anxious faces. Some of the children had begun to weep. Women offered loud suggestions. There were surmises that Bobby had been run over by a cart in the street, and angry conjectures that he had been stolen. Then Ailie wailed:

"Oh, Maister Traill, the bittie dog's deid!"

"Havers, lassie! I'm ashamed o' ye for a fulish bairn. Bobby's no' deid. Nae doot he's amang the stanes i' the kirkyaird. He's aye scramblin' aboot for vermin an' pussies, an' may hae hurt himsel', an' ye a' ken the bonny wee wadna cry oot i' the kirkyaird. Noo, get to wark, an' dinna stand there greetin' an' waggin' yer tongues. The mithers an' bairns maun juist gang hame an' stap their havers, an' licht a' the candles an' cruisey lamps i' their hames, an' set them i' the windows aboon the kirkyaird. Greyfriars is murky by the ordinar', an' ye couldna find a coo there wi'oot the lichts."

The crowd suddenly melted away, so eager were they all to have a hand in helping to find the community pet. Then Mr. Traill turned to the boys.

"Hoo mony o' ye laddies hae the bull's-eye
lanterns?"

Ah! not many in the old buildings around the
kirkyard. These japanned tin aids to dark adventures on the golf links on autumn nights cost
a sixpence and consumed candles. Geordie Ross
and Sandy McGregor, coming up arm in arm,
knew of other students and clerks who still had
these cherished toys of boyhood. With these
heroes in the lead a score or more of laddies
swarmed into the kirkyard.

The tenements were lighted up as they had
not been since nobles held routs and balls there.
Enough candles and oil were going up in smoke
to pay for wee Bobby's license all over again, and
enough love shone in pallid little faces that
peered into the dusk to light the darkest corner
in the heart of the world. Rays from the bull's-
eyes were thrown into every nook and cranny.
Very small laddies insinuated themselves into
the narrowest places. They climbed upon high
vaults and let themselves down in last year's
burdocks and tangled vines. It was all done in
silence, only Mr. Traill speaking at all. He went
everywhere with the searchers, and called:

"Whaur are ye, Bobby? Come awa' oot,
laddie!"

But no gleaming ghost of a tousled dog was

conjured by the voice of affection. The tiniest scratching or lowest moaning could have been heard, for the warm spring evening was very still, and there were, as yet, few leaves to rustle. Sleepy birds complained at being disturbed on their perches, and rodents could be heard scampering along their runways. The entire kirkyard was explored, then the interior of the two kirks. Mr. Traill went up to the lodge for the keys, saying, optimistically, that a sexton might unwittingly have locked Bobby in. Young men with lanterns went through the courts of the tenements, around the Grassmarket, and under the arches of the bridge. Laddies dropped from the wall and hunted over Heriot's Hospital grounds to Lauriston market. Tammy, poignantly conscious of being of no practical use, sat on Auld Jock's grave, firm in the conviction that Bobby would return to that spot his ainsel'. And Ailie, being only a maid, whose portion it was to wait and weep, lay across the window-sill, on the pediment of the tomb, a limp little figure of woe.

Mr. Traill's heart was full of misgiving. Nothing but death or stone walls could keep that little creature from this beloved grave. But, in thinking of stone walls, he never once thought of the Castle. Away over to the east, in Broughton

market, when the garrison marched away and at
Lauriston when they returned, Mr. Traill did not
know that the soldiers had been out of the city.
Busy in the lodge Mistress Jeanie had not seen
them go by the kirkyard, and no one else, except
Mr. Brown, knew the fascination that military
uniforms, marching and music had for wee Bobby.

A fog began to drift in from the sea. Suddenly the grass was sheeted and the tombs
blurred. A curtain of gauze seemed to be hung
before the lighted tenements. The Castle head
vanished, and the sounds of the drum and bugle
of the tattoo came down muffled, as if through
layers of wool. The lights of the bull's-eyes were
ruddy discs that cast no rays. Ther these were
smeared out to phosphorescent glows, like the
"spunkies" that everybody in Scotland knew
came out to dance in old kirkyards.

It was no' canny. In the smother of the fog
some of the little boys were lost, and cried out.
Mr. Traill got them up to the gate and sent them
home in bands, under the escort of the students.
Mistress Jeanie was out by the wicket. Mr.
Brown was asleep, and she " couldna thole it to
sit there snug." When a fog-horn moaned from
the Firth she broke into sobbing. Mr. Traill
comforted her as best he could by telling her a
dozen plans for the morning. By feeling along

the wall he got her to the lodge, and himself up to his cozy dining-rooms.

For the first time since Queen Mary the gate of the historic garden of the Greyfriars was left on the latch. And it was so that a little dog, coming home in the night. might not be shut out

XI

IT was more than two hours after he left
Bobby in Queen Margaret's Chapel that the
sergeant turned into the officers' mess-room and
tried to get an orderly to take a message to the
captain who had noticed the little dog in the
barracks. He wished to report that Bobby
could not be found, and to be excused to continue
the search.

He had to wait by the door while the toast to
her Majesty was proposed and the band in the
screened gallery broke into "God Save the
Queen"; and when the music stopped the bandmaster came in for the usual compliments.

The evening was so warm and still, although it
was only mid-April, that a glass - paneled door,
opening on the terrace, was set ajar for air.
In the confusion of movement and talk no one
noticed a little black mop of a muzzle that was
poked through the aperture. From the outer
darkness Bobby looked in on the score or more
of men doubtfully, ready for instant disappearance on the slightest alarm. Desperate was the

emergency, forlorn the hope that had brought him there. At every turn his efforts to escape from the Castle had been baffled. He had been imprisoned by drummer boys and young recruits in the gymnasium, detained in the hospital, captured in the canteen.

Bobby went through all his pretty tricks for the lads, and then begged to be let go. Laughed at, romped with, dragged back, thrown into the swimming-pool, expected to play and perform for them, he rebelled at last. He scarred the door with his claws, and he howled so dismally that, hearing an orderly corporal coming, they turned him out in a rough haste that terrified him. In the old Banqueting Hall on the Palace Yard, that was used as a hospital and dispensary, he went through that travesty of joy again, in hope of the reward.

Sharply rebuked and put out of the hospital, at last, because of his destructive clawing and mournful howling, Bobby dashed across the Palace Yard and into a crowd of good-humored soldiers who lounged in the canteen. Rising on his hind legs to beg for attention and indulgence, he was taken unaware from behind by an admiring soldier who wanted to romp with him. Quite desperate by that time, he snapped at the hand of his captor and sprang away into the first

dark opening. Frightened by the man's cry of
pain, and by the calls and scuffling search for him
without, he slunk to the farthest corner of a
dungeon of the Middle Ages, under the Royal
Lodging.

When the hunt for him ceased, Bobby slipped
out of hiding and made his way around the
sickle-shaped ledge of rock, and under the guns
of the half-moon battery, to the outer gate.
Only a cat, a fox, or a low, weasel-like dog could
have done it. There were many details that
would have enabled the observant little creature
to recognize this barrier as the place where he
had come in. Certainly he attacked it with fury,
and on the guards he lavished every art of appeal
that he possessed. But there he was bantered,
and a feint was made of shutting him up in the
guard-house as a disorderly person. With a
heart-broken cry he escaped his tormentors, and
made his way back, under the guns, to the citadel.

His confidence in the good intentions of men
shaken, Bobby took to furtive ways. Avoiding
lighted buildings and voices, he sped from shadow
to shadow and explored the walls of solid masonry. Again and again he returned to the postern behind the armory, but the small back gate
that gave to the cliff was not opened. Once he
scrambled up to a loophole in the fortifications

and looked abroad at the scattered lights of the city set in the void of night. But there, indeed, his stout heart failed him.

It was not long before Bobby discovered that he was being pursued. A number of soldiers and drummer boys were out hunting for him, contritely enough, when the situation was explained by the angry sergeant. Wherever he went voices and footsteps followed. Had the sergeant gone alone and called in familiar speech, "Come awa' oot, Bobby!" he would probably have run to the man. But there were so many calls—in English, in Celtic, and in various dialects of the Lowlands —that the little dog dared not trust them. From place to place he was driven by fear, and when the calling stopped and the footsteps no longer followed, he lay for a time where he could watch the postern. A moment after he gave up the vigil there the little back gate was opened.

Desperation led him to take another chance with men. Slipping into the shadow of the old Governor's House, the headquarters of commissioned officers, on the terrace above the barracks, he lay near the open door to the mess-room, listening and watching.

The pretty ceremony of toasting the bandmaster brought all the company about the table again, and the polite pause in the conversation on his exit, gave an opportunity for the captain to speak of Bobby before the sergeant could get his message delivered.

"Gentlemen, your indulgence for a moment, to drink another toast to a little dog that is said to have slept on his master's grave in Greyfriars churchyard for more than eight years. Sergeant Scott, of the Royal Engineers, vouches for the story and will present the hero."

The sergeant came forward then with the word that Bobby could not be found. He was somewhere in the Castle, and had made persistent and frantic efforts to get out. Prevented at every turn, and forcibly held in various places by well-meaning but blundering soldiers, he had been frightened into hiding.

Bobby heard every word, and he must have understood that he himself was under discussion. Alternately hopeful and apprehensive, he scanned each face in the room that came within range of his vision, until one arrested and drew him. Such faces, full of understanding, love and compassion for dumb animals, are to be found among men, women and children, in any company and in every corner of the world. Now, with the dog's instinct for the dog-lover, Bobby made his way about the room unnoticed, and set his short, shagged paws up on this man's knee.

GREYFRIARS BOBBY

"Bless my soul, gentlemen, here's the little dog now, and a beautiful specimen of the drop-eared Skye he is. Why didn't you say that the 'bittie' dog was of the Highland breed, Sergeant? You may well believe any extravagant tale you may hear of the fidelity and affection of the Skye terrier."

And with that wee Bobby was set upon the polished table, his own silver image glimmering among the reflections of candles and old plate. He kept close under the hand of his protector, but waiting for the moment favorable to his appeal. The company crowded around with eager interest, while the man of expert knowledge and love of dogs talked about Bobby.

"You see he's a well-knit little rascal, long and low, hardy and strong. His ancestors were bred for bolting foxes and wildcats among the rocky headlands of the subarctic islands. The intelligence, courage and devotion of dogs of this breed can scarcely be overstated. There is some far-away crossing here that gives this one a greater beauty and grace and more engaging manners, making him a 'sport' among rough farm dogs—but look at the length and strength of the muzzle. He's as determined as the deil. You would have to break his neck before you could break his purpose. For love of his master he would starve, or he would leap to his death without an instant's hesitation."

All this time the man had been stroking Bobby's head and neck. Now, feeling the collar under the thatch, he slipped it out and brought the brass plate up to the light.

"Propose your toast to Greyfriars Bobby, Captain. His story is vouched for by no less a person than the Lord Provost. The 'bittie' dog seems to have won a sort of canine Victoria Cross."

The toast was drunk standing, and a cheer given. The company pressed close to examine the collar and to shake Bobby's lifted paw. Then, thinking the moment had come, Bobby rose in the begging attitude, prostrated himself before them, and uttered a pleading cry. His new friend assured him that he would be taken home.

"Bide a wee, Bobby. Before he goes I want you all to see his beautiful eyes. In most breeds of dogs with the veil you will find the hairs of the face discolored by tears, but the Skye terrier's are not, and his eyes are living jewels, as sunny a brown as cairngorms in pebble brooches, but soft and deep and with an almost human intelligence."

For the third time that day Bobby's veil was

pushed back. One shocked look by this lover of dogs, and it was dropped.

"Get him back to that grave, man, or he's like to die. His eyes are just two cairngorms of grief."

In the hush that fell upon the company the senior officer spoke sharply: "Take him down at once, Sergeant. The whole affair is most unfortunate, and you will please tender my apologies at the churchyard and the restaurant, as well as your own, and I will see the Lord Provost."

The military salute was given to Bobby when he leaped from the table at the sergeant's call: "Come awa', Bobby. I'll tak' ye to Auld Jock i' the kirkyaird noo."

He stepped out onto the lawn to wait for his pass. Bobby stood at his feet, quivering with impatience to be off, but trusting in the man's given word. The upper air was clear, and the sky studded with stars. Twenty minutes before the May Light, that guided the ships into the Firth, could be seen far out on the edge of the ocean, and in every direction the lamps of the city seemed to fall away in a shower of sparks, as from a burst meteor. But now, while the stars above were as numerous and as brilliant as before, the lights below had vanished. As

the sergeant looked, the highest ones expired in
the rising fog. The Island Rock appeared to be
sinking in a waveless sea of milk.

A startled exclamation from the sergeant
brought other men out on the terrace to see it.
The senior officer withheld the pass in his hand,
and scouted the idea of the sergeant's going
down into the city. As the drum began to beat
the tattoo and the bugle to rise on a crescendo of
lovely notes, soldiers swarmed toward the barracks. Those who had been out in the town
came running up the roadway into the Castle,
talking loudly of adventures they had had in
the fog. The sergeant looked down at anxious
Bobby, who stood agitated and straining as at a
leash, and said that he preferred to go.

"Impossible! A foolish risk, Sergeant, that I
am unwilling you should take. Edinburgh is too
full of pitfalls for a man to be going about on
such a night. Our guests will sleep in the Castle,
and it will be safer for the little dog to remain
until morning."

Bobby did not quite understand this good
English, but the excited talk and the delay
made him uneasy. He whimpered piteously. He
lay across the sergeant's feet, and through his
boots the man could feel the little creature's
heart beat. Then he rose and uttered his plead-

ing cry. The sergeant stooped and patted the shaggy head consolingly, and tried to explain matters.

"Be a gude doggie noo. Dinna fash yersel' aboot what canna be helped. I canna tak' ye to the kirkyaird the nicht."

"I'll take charge of Bobby, Sergeant." The dog-loving guest ran out hastily, but, with a wild cry of reproach and despair, Bobby was gone.

The group of soldiers who had been out on the cliff were standing in the postern a moment to look down at the opaque flood that was rising around the rock. They felt some flying thing sweep over their feet and caught a silvery flash of it across the promenade. The sergeant cried to them to stop the dog, and he and the guest were out in time to see Bobby go over the precipice.

For a time the little dog lay in a clump of hazel above the fog, between two terrors. He could see the men and the lights moving along the top of the cliff, and he could hear the calls. Some one caught a glimpse of him, and the sergeant lay down on the edge of the precipice and talked to him, saying every kind and foolish thing he could think of to persuade Bobby to come back. Then a drummer boy was tied to a rope and let down to the ledge to fetch him up

But at that, without any sound at all, Bobby dropped out of sight.

Through the smother came the loud moaning of fog - horns in the Firth. Although nothing could be seen, and sounds were muffled as if the ears of the world were stuffed with wool, odors were held captive and mingled in confusion. There was nothing to guide a little dog's nose, everything to make him distrust his most reliable sense. The smell of every plant on the crag was there; the odors of leather, of paint, of wood, of iron, from the crafts shops at the base. Smoke from chimneys in the valley was mixed with the strong scent of horses, hay and grain from the street of King's Stables. There was the smell of furry rodents, of nesting birds, of gushing springs, of the earth itself, and something more ancient still, as of burned-out fires in the huge mass of trap-rock.

Everything warned Bobby to lie still in safety until morning and the world was restored to its normal aspects. But ah! in the highest type of man and dog, self-sacrifice, and not self-preservation, is the first law. A deserted grave cried to him across the void, the anguish of protecting love urged him on to take perilous chances. Falling upon a narrow shelf of rock, he had bounded off and into a thicket of thorns. Bruised and shaken and bewildered, he lay there for a time and tried to get his bearings.

Bobby knew only that the way was downward. He put out a paw and felt for the edge of the shelf. A thorn bush rooted below tickled his nose. He dropped into that and scrambled out again. Loose earth broke under his struggles and carried him swiftly down to a new level. He slipped in the wet moss of a spring before he heard the tinkle of the water, lost his foothold, and fell against a sharp point of rock. The shadowy spire of a fir-tree looming in a parting of the vapor for an instant, Bobby leaped to the ledge upon which it was rooted.

Foot by foot he went down, with no guidance at all. It is the nature of such long, low, earth dogs to go by leaps and bounds like foxes, calculating distances nicely when they can see, and tearing across the roughest country with the speed of the wild animals they hunt. And where the way is very steep they can scramble up or down any declivity that is at a lesser angle than the perpendicular. Head first they go downward, setting the fore paws forward, the claws clutching around projections and in fissures, the weight hung from the stout hind quarters, the body flattened on the earth.

Thus Bobby crept down steep descents in safety.

but his claws were broken in crevices and his feet were torn and pierced by splinters of rock and thorns. Once he went some distance into a cave and had to back up and out again. And then a promising slope shelving under suddenly, where he could not retreat, he leaped, turned over and over in the air, and fell stunned. His heart filled with fear of the unseen before him, the little dog lay for a long time in a clump of whins. He may even have dozed and dreamed, to be awakened with starts by his misery of longing, and once by the far-away barking of a dog. It came up deadened, as if from fathoms below. He stood up and listened, but the sound was not repeated. His lacerated feet burned and throbbed; his bruised muscles had begun to stiffen, so that every movement was a pain.

In these lower levels there was more smoke, that smeared out and thickened the mist. Suddenly a breath of air parted the fog as if it were a torn curtain. Like a shot Bobby went down the crag, leaping from rock to rock, scrambling under thorns and hazel shrubs, dropping over precipitous ledges, until he looked down a sheer fall on which not even a knot of grass could find a foothold. He took the leap instantly, and his thick fleece saved him from broken bones; but when he tried to get up again his body was

racked with pain and his hind legs refused to
serve him.

Turning swiftly, he snarled and bit at them in
angry disbelief that his good little legs should
play false with his stout heart. Then he quite
forgot his pain, for there was the sharp ring of
iron on an anvil and the dull glow of a forge
fire, where a smith was toiling in the early hours
of the morning. A clever and resourceful little
dog, Bobby made shift to do without legs.
Turning on his side, he rolled down the last slope
of Castle Rock. Crawling between two buildings
and dropping from the terrace on which they
stood, he fell into a little street at the west end
and above the Grassmarket.

Here the odors were all of the stables. He
knew the way, and that it was still downward.
The distance he had to go was a matter of a
quarter of a mile, or less, and the greater part of
it was on the level, through the sunken valley of
the Grassmarket. But Bobby had literally to
drag himself now; and he had still to pull himself up by his fore paws over the wet and greasy
cobblestones of Candlemakers Row. Had not
the great leaves of the gate to the kirkyard
been left on the latch, he would have had to lie
there in the alcove, with his nose under the bars,
until morning. But the gate gave way to his

push, and so, he dragged himself through it and around the kirk, and stretched himself on Auld Jock's grave.

It was the birds that found him there in the misty dawn. They were used to seeing Bobby scampering about, for the little watchman was awake and busy as early as the feathered dwellers in the kirkyard. But, in what looked to be a wet and furry door-mat left out overnight on the grass, they did not know him at all. The throstles and skylarks were shy of it, thinking it might be alive. The wrens fluffed themselves, scolded it, and told it to get up. The blue titmice flew over it in a flock again and again, with much sweet gossiping, but they did not venture nearer. A redbreast lighted on the rose bush that marked Auld Jock's grave, cocked its head knowingly, and warbled a little song, as much as to say: "If it's alive that will wake it up."

As Bobby did not stir, the robin fluttered down, studied him from all sides, made polite inquiries that were not answered, and concluded that it would be quite safe to take a silver hair for nest lining. Then, startled by the animal warmth or by a faint, breathing movement, it dropped the shining trophy and flew away in a shrill panic. At that, all the birds set up such an excited crying that they waked Tammy.

From the rude loophole of a window that projected from the old Cunzie Neuk, the crippled laddie could see only the shadowy tombs and the long gray wall of the two kirks, through the sunny haze. But he dropped his crutches over, and climbed out onto the vault. Never before had Bobby failed to hear that well-known tap-tap-tapping on the graveled path, nor failed to trot down to meet it with friskings of welcome. But now he lay very still, even when a pair of frail arms tried to lift his dead weight to a heaving breast, and Tammy's cry of woe rang through the kirkyard. In a moment Ailie and Mistress Jeanie were in the wet grass beside them, half a hundred casements flew open, and the piping voices of tenement bairns cried down:

"Did the bittie doggie come hame?"

Oh yes, the bittie doggie had come hame, indeed, but down such perilous heights as none of them d eamed; and now in what a woeful plight!

Some murmur of the excitement reached an open dormer of the Temple tenements, where Geordie Ross had slept with one ear of the born doctor open. Snatching up a case of first aids to the injured, he ran down the twisting stairs to the Grassmarket, up to the gate, and around the kirk, to find a huddled group of women and children weeping over a limp little bundle of a senseless dog. He thrust a bottle of hartshorn under the black muzzle, and with a start and a moan Bobby came back to consciousness.

"Lay him down flat and stop your havers," ordered the business-like, embryo medicine man. "Bobby's no' dead. Laddie, you're a braw soldier for holding your ain feelings, so just hold the wee dog's head." Then, in the reassuring dialect: "Hoots, Bobby, open the bit mou' noo, an' tak' the medicine like a mannie!" Down the tiny red cavern of a throat Geordie poured a dose that galvanized the small creature into life.

"Noo. :hen, loup, ye bonny rascal!"

Bobby did his best to jump at Geordie's bidding. He was so glad to be at home and to see all these familiar faces of love that he lifted himself on his fore paws, and his happy heart almost put the power to loup into his hind legs. But when he tried to stand up he cried out with the pains and sank down again, with an apologetic and shamefaced look that was worthy of Auld Jock himself. Geordie sobered on the instant.

"Weel, now, he's been hurt. We'll just have to see what ails the sonsie doggie." He ran his hand down the parting in the thatch to discover if the spine had been injured. When he suddenly pinched the ball of a hind toe Bobby promptly resented it by jerking his head around and looking at him reproachfully. The bairns were indignant, too, but Geordie grinned cheerfully and said: "He's no' paralyzed, at ony rate." He turned as footsteps were heard coming hastily around the kirk.

"A gude morning to you, Mr. Traill. Bobby may have been run over by a cart and got internal injuries, but I'm thinking it's just sprains and bruises from a bad fall. He was in a state of collapse, and his claws are as broken and his toes as torn as if he had come down Castle Rock."

This was such an extravagant surmise that even the anxious landlord smiled. Then he said, drily:

"You're a braw laddie, Geordie, and gude-hearted, but you're no' a doctor yet, and, with your leave, I'll have my ain medical man tak' a look at Bobby."

"Ay, I would," Geordie agreed, cordially. "It's worth four shullings to have your mind at ease, man. I'll just go up to the lodge and get a warm bath ready, to tak' the stiffness out of his muscles, and brew a tea from an herb that wee wild creatures know all about and aye hunt for when they're ailing."

Geordie went away gaily, to take disorder and evil smells into Mistress Jeanie's shining kitchen

No sooner had the medical student gone up to the lodge, and the children had been persuaded to go home to watch the proceedings anxiously from the amphitheater of the tenement windows, than the kirkyard gate was slammed back noisily by a man in a hurry. It was the sergeant who, in the splendor of full uniform, dropped in the wet grass beside Bobby.

"Losh! The sma' dog got hame, an' is still leevin'. Noo, God forgie me—"

"Eh, man, what had you to do with Bobby's misadventure?"

Mr. Traill fixed an accusing eye on the soldier, remembering suddenly his laughing threat to kidnap Bobby. The story came out in a flood of remorseful words, from Bobby's following of the troops so gaily into the Castle to his desperate escape over the precipice.

"Noo," he said, humbly, "gin it wad be ony satisfaction to ye, I'll gang up to the Castle an' put on fatigue-dress, no' to disgrace the unifarm o' her Maijesty, an' let ye tak' me oot on the Burghmuir an' gie me a gude lickin'."

Mr. Traill shrugged his shoulders. "Naething would satisfy me, man, but to get behind you and kick you over the Firth into the Kingdom of Fife."

He turned an angry back on the sergeant and

helped Geordie lift Bobby onto Mrs. Brown's braided hearth-rug and carry the improvised litter up to the lodge. In the kitchen the little dog was lowered into a hot bath, dried, and rubbed with liniments under his fleece. After his lacerated feet had been cleaned and dressed with healing ointments and tied up, Bobby was wrapped in Mistress Jeanie's best flannel petticoat and laid on the hearth-rug, a very comfortable wee dog, who enjoyed his breakfast of broth and porridge.

Mr. Brown, hearing the commotion and perishing of curiosity, demanded that some one should come and help him out of bed. As no attention was paid to him he managed to get up himself and to hobble out to the kitchen just as Mr. Traill's ain medical man came in. Bobby's spine was examined again, the tail and toes nipped, the heart tested, and all the soft parts of his body pressed and punched, in spite of the little dog's vigorous objections to these indignities.

"Except for sprains and bruises the wee dog is all right. Came down Castle Crag in the fog, did he? He's a clever and plucky little chap, indeed, and deserving of a hero medal to hang on the Lord Provost's collar. You've done very well, Mr. Ross. Just take as good care of him for a week or so and he could do the gallant deed again."

Mr. Brown listened to the story of Bobby's adventures with a mingled look of disgust at the foolishness of men, pride in Bobby's prowess, and resentment at having been left out of the drama of the night before. "It's maist michty, noo, Maister Traill, that ye wad tak' the leeberty o' leein' to me," he complained.

"It was a gude lee or a bad nicht for an ill man. Geordie will tell you that a mind at ease is worth four shullings, and I'm charging you naething. Eh, man, you're deeficult to please." As he went out into the kirkyard Mr. Traill stopped to reflect on a strange thing: "'You've done very well, Mr. Ross.' Weel, weel, how the laddies do grow up! But I'm no' going to admit it to Geordie."

Another thought, over which he chuckled, sent him off to find the sergeant. The soldier was tramping gloomily about in the wet, to the demoralization of his beautiful boots.

"Man, since a stormy nicht eight years ago last November I've aye been looking for a bigger weel-meaning fule than my ain sel'. You're the man, so if you'll just shak' hands we'll say nae more about it."

He did not explain this cryptic remark, but he went on to assure the sorry soldier that Bobby had got no serious hurt and would soon be as well as ever. They had turned toward the gate when a stranger with a newspaper in his hand peered mildly around the kirk and inquired: "Do ye ken whaur's the sma' dog, man?" As Mr. Traill continued to stare at him he explained, patiently: "It's Greyfriars Bobby, the bittie terrier the Laird Provost gied the collar to. Hae ye no' seen *The Scotsman* the day?"

The landlord had not. And there was the story, Bobby's name heading quite a quarter of a broad column of fine print, and beginning with: "A very singular and interesting occurrence was brought to light in the Burgh court by the hearing of a summons in regard to a dog tax." Bobby was a famous dog, and Mr. Traill came in for a goodly portion of reflected glory. He threw up his hands in dismay.

"It's all over the toon, Sergeant." Turning to the stranger, he assured him that Bobby was not to be seen. "He hurt himsel' coming down Castle Rock in the nicht, and is in the lodge with the caretaker, wha's fair ill. Hoo do I ken?" testily. "Wee', man, I'm Mr. Traill."

He saw at once how unwise was that admission, for he had to shake hands with the cordial stranger. And after dismissing him there was another at the gate who insisted upon going up to the lodge to see the little hero. Here was a state of things, indeed, that called upon all the powers of the resourceful landlord.

"All the folk in Edinburgh will be coming, and the poor woman be deaved with their spiering." And then he began to laugh. "Did you ever hear o' sic a thing as poetic justice, Sergeant? Nae, it's no' the kind you'll get in the courts of law. Weel, it's poetic justice for a birkie soldier, wha claims the airth and the fullness thereof, to have to tak' his orders from a sma' shopkeeper. Go up to the police office in St. Giles now and ask for an officer to stand at the gate here to answer queistions, and to keep the folk awa' from the lodge."

He stood guard himself, and satisfied a score of visitors before the sergeant came back, and there was another instance of poetic justice, in the crestfallen Burgh policeman who had been sent with instructions to take his orders from the delighted landlord.

"Eh, Davie, it's a lang lane that has nae turning. Ye're juist to stand here a' the day an' say to ilka body wha spiers for the dog: 'Ay, sir, Greyfriars Bobby's been leevin' i' the kirkyaird aucht years an' mair, an' Maister Traill's aye fed 'im i' the dining-rooms. Ay, the case was dismissed i' the Burgh coort. The Laird Provost

gied a collar to the bit Skye because there's a
meddlin' fule or twa amang the Burgh police
wha'd be takin' 'im up. The doggie's i' the
lodge wi' the caretaker, wha's fair ill, an' he
canna be seen the day. But gang aroond the
kirk an' ye can see Auld Jock's grave that he's
aye guarded. There's nae stane to it, but it's
neist to the fa'en table-tomb o' Mistress Jean
Grant. A gude day to ye.' Hae ye got a' that,
man? Weel, cheer up. Ye'll hae to say it nae
mair than a thousand times or twa atween noo
an' nichtfa'."

He went away laughing at the penance that
was laid upon his foe. The landlord felt so well
satisfied with the world that he took another
jaunty crack at the sergeant: "By richts, man,
you ought to go to gaol, but I'll just fine you a
shulling a month for Bobby's natural lifetime, to
give the wee soldier a treat of a steak or a chop
once a week."

Hands were struck heartily on the bargain, and
the two men parted good friends. Now, finding
Ailie dropping tears in the dish-water, Mr. Traill
sent her flying down to the lodge with instructions
to make herself useful to Mrs. Brown. Then he
was himself besieged in his place of business by
folk of high and low degree who were disappointed by their failure to see Bobby in the

kirkyard. Greyfriars Dining-Rooms had more distinguished visitors in a day than they had had in all the years since Auld Jock died and a little dog fell there at the landlord's feet "a' but deid wi' hunger."

Not one of all the grand folk who inquired for Bobby at the kirkyard or at the restaurant got a glimpse of him that day. But after they were gone the tenement dwellers came up to the gate again, as they had gthered the evening before, and begged that they might just tak' a look at him and his braw collar.

"The bonny bit is the bairns' ain doggie, an' the Laird Provost himsel' told 'em he wasna to be neglectet," was one mother's plea.

Ah! that was very true. To the grand folk who had come to see him, Bobby was only a nine-days' wonder. His story had touched the hearts of all orders of society. For a time strangers would come to see him, and then they would forget all about him or remember him only fitfully. It was to these poor people around the kirkyard, themselves forgotten by the more fortunate, that the little dog must look for his daily meed of affection and companionship. Mr. Traill spoke to them kindly.

"Bide a wee, noo, an' I'll fetch the doggie doon."

Bobby had slept blissfully nearly all the day, after his exhausting labors and torturing pains. But with the sunset bugle he fretted to be let out. Ailie had wept and pleaded, Mrs. Brown had reasoned with him, and Mr. Brown had scolded, all to the end of persuading him to sleep in "the hoose the nicht." But when no one was watching him Bobby crawled from his rug and dragged himself to the door. He rapped the floor with his tail in delight when Mr. Traill came in and bundled him up on the rug, so he could lie easily, and carried him down to the gate.

For quite twenty minutes these neighbors and friends of Bobby filed by silently, patted the shaggy little head, looked at the grand plate with Bobby's and the Lord Provost's names upon it, and believed their own wondering een. Bobby wagged his tail and lolled his tongue, and now and then he licked the hand of a baby who had to be lifted by a tall brother to see him. Shy kisses were dropped on Bobby's head by toddling bairns, and awkward caresses by rough laddies. Then they all went home quietly, and Mr. Traill carried the little dog around the kirk.

And there, ah! so belated, Auld Jock's grave bore its tribute of flowers. Wreaths and nosegays, potted daffodils and primroses and daisies, covered the sunken mound so that some of them had to be moved to make room for Bobby. He sniffed and sniffed at them, looked up inquiringly at Mr. Traill, and then snuggled down contentedly among the blossoms. He did not understand their being there any more than he understood the collar about which everybody made such a to-do. The narrow band of leather would disappear under his thatch again, and would be unnoticed by the casual passer-by; the flowers would fade and never be so lavishly renewed; but there was another more wonderful gift, now, that would never fail him.

At nightfall, before the drum and bugle sounded the tattoo to call the scattered garrison in the Castle, there took place a loving ceremony that was never afterward omitted as long as Bobby lived. Every child newly come to the tenements learned it, every weanie lisped it among his first words. Before going to bed each bairn opened a casement. Sometimes a candle was held up—a little star of love, glimmering for a moment on the dark; but always there was a small face peering into the melancholy kirkyard. In midsummer, and at other seasons if the moon rose full and early and the sky was clear, Bobby could be seen on the grave. And when he recovered from these hurts he trotted about. making the circuit below the windows.

He could not speak there, because he had been forbidden, but he could wag his tail and look up to show his friendliness. And whether the children saw him or not they knew he was always there after sunset, keeping watch and ward, and "lanely" because his master had gone away to heaven; and so they called out to him sweetly and clearly:

"A gude nicht to ye, Bobby."

XII

IN one thing Mr. Traill had been mistaken
the grand folk did not forget Bobby. At
the end of five years the leal Highlander was not
only still remembered, but he had become a local
celebrity.

Had the grave of his haunting been on the
Pentlands or in one of the outlying cemeteries of
the city Bobby must have been known to few
of his generation, and to fame not at all. But
among churchyards Greyfriars was distinguished.
One of the historic show-places of Edinburgh,
and in the very heart of the Old Town, it was
never missed by the most hurried tourist, seldom
left unvisited, from year to year, by the oldest
resident. Names on its old tombs had come to
mean nothing to those who read them, except as
they recalled memorable records of love, of inspiration, of courage, of self-sacrifice. And this
being so, it touched the imagination to see,
among the marbles that crumbled toward the
dust below, a living embodiment of affection and
fidelity. Indeed, it came to be remarked, as it is

remarked to-day, although four decades have gone by, that no other spot in Greyfriars was so much cared for as the grave of a man of whom nothing was known except that the life and love of a little dog was consecrated to his memory.

At almost any hour Bobby might be found there. As he grew older he became less and less willing to be long absent, and he got much of his exercise by nosing about among the neighboring thorns. In fair weather he took his frequent naps on the turf above his master, or he sat on the fallen table-tomb in the sun. On foul days he watched the grave from under the slab, and to that spot he returned from every skirmish against the enemy. Visitors stopped to speak to him. Favored ones were permitted to read the inscription on his collar and to pat his head. It seemed, therefore, the most natural thing in the world when the greatest lady in England, beside the Queen, the Baroness Burdett-Coutts, came all the way from London to see Bobby.

Except that it was the first Monday in June, and Founder's Day at Heriot's Hospital, it was like any other day of useful work, innocent pleasure, and dreaming dozes on Auld Jock's grave to wee Bobby. As years go, the shaggy little Skye was an old dog, but he was not feeble or blind or unhappy. A terrier, as a rule, does

not live as long as more sluggish breeds of dogs,
but, active to the very end, he literally wears
himself out tearing around, and then goes, little
soldier, very suddenly, dying gallantly with his
boots on.

In the very early mornings of the northern
summer Bobby woke with the birds, a long time
before the reveille was sounded from the Castle.
He scampered down to the circling street of
tombs at once and not until the last prowler had
been despatched, or frightened into his burrow,
did he return for a brief nap on Auld Jock's grave.

All about him the birds fluttered and hopped
and gossiped and foraged, unafraid. They were
used, by this time, to seeing the little dog lying
motionless, his nose on his paws. Often some
tidbit of food lay there, brought for Bobby by a
stranger. He had learned that a Scotch bun
dropped near him was a feast that brought
feathered visitors about and won their confidence
and cheerful companionship. When he awoke
he lay there lolling and blinking, following the
blue rovings of the titmice and listening to the
foolish squabbles of the sparrows and the shrew-
ish scoldings of the wrens. He always started
when a lark sprang at his feet and a cataract of
melody tumbled from the sky.

But, best of all, Bobby loved a comfortable

and friendly robin redbreast—not the American thrush that is called a robin, but the smaller Old World warbler. It had its nest of grass and moss and feathers, and many a silver hair shed by Bobby, low in a near-by thorn bush. In sweet and plaintive talking notes it told its little dog companion all about the babies that had left the nest and the new brood that would soon be there. On the morning of that wonderful day of the Grand Leddy's first coming, Bobby and the redbreast had a pleasant visit together before the casements began to open and the tenement bairns called down their morning greeting:

"A gude day to ye, Bobby."

By the time all these courtesies had been returned Tammy came in at the gate with his college books strapped on his back. The old Cunzie Neuk had been demolished by Glenormiston, and Tammy, living in better quarters, was studying to be a teacher at Heriot's. Bobby saw him settled, and then he had to escort Mr. Brown down from the lodge. The caretaker made his way about stiffly with a cane and, with the aid of a young helper who exasperated the old gardener by his cheerful inefficiency, kept the auld kirkyard in beautiful order.

"Eh, ye gude-for-naethin' tyke," he said to Bobby, in transparent pretense of his uselessness.

"Get to wark, or I'll hae a young dog in to gie ye a lift, an' syne whaur 'll ye be?"

Bobby jumped on him in open delight at this, as much as to say: "Ye may be as dour as ye like, but ilka body kens ye're gude-hearted."

Morning and evening numerous friends passed the gate, and the wee dog waited for them on the wicket. Dr. George Ross and Mr. Alexander McGregor shook Bobby's lifted paw and called him a sonsie rascal. Small merchants, students, clerks, factory workers, house servants, laborers and vendors, all honest and useful people, had come up out of these old tenements within Bobby's memory; and others had gone down, alas! into the Cowgate. But Bobby's tail wagged for these unfortunates, too, and some of them had no other friend in the world beside that uncalculating little dog.

When the morning stream of auld acquaintance had gone by, and none forgot, Bobby went up to the lodge to sit for an hour with Mistress Jeanie. There he was called "croodlin' doo"—which was altogether absurd—by the fond old woman. As neat of plumage, and as busy and talkative about small domestic matters as the robin, Bobby loved to watch the wifie stirring savory messes over the fire, watering her posies, cleaning the fluttering skylark's cage, or just sitting

by the hearth or in the sunny doorway with
him, knitting warm stockings for her rheumatic
gude-mon.

Out in the kirkyard Bobby trotted dutifully
at the caretaker's heels. When visitors were
about he did not venture to take a nap in the
open unless Mr. Brown was on guard, and,
by long and close companionship with him, the
aging man could often tell what Bobby was
dreaming about. At a convulsive movement and
a jerk of his head the caretaker would say to the
wifie, if she chanced to be near:

"Leuk at that, noo, wull ye? The sperity bit
was takin' thae fou' vermin." And again, when
the muscles of his legs worked rhythmically,
"He's rinnin' wi' the laddies or the braw soldiers
on the braes."

Bobby often woke from a dream with a start,
looked dazed, and then foolish, at the vivid
imaginings of sleep. But when, in a doze, he
half stretched himself up on his short, shagged
fore paws, flattened out, and then awoke and lay
so, very still, for a time, it was Mistress Jeanie
who said:

"Preserve us a'! The bonny wee was dreamin'
o' his maister's deith, an' noo he's greetin' sair."

At that she took her little stool and sat on the
grave beside him. But Mr. Brown bit his teeth

GREYFRIARS BOBBY

in his pipe, limped away, and stormed at his daft
helper laddie, who didn't appear to know a violet
from a burdock.

Ah! who can doubt that, so deeply were scene
and word graven on his memory, Bobby often
lived again the hour of his bereavement, and
heard Auld Jock's last words:

"Gang—awa'—hame—laddie!"

Homeless on earth, gude Auld Jock had gone
to a place prepared for him. But his faithful
little dog had no home. This sacred spot was
merely his tarrying place, where he waited until
such a time as that mysterious door should open
for him, perchance to an equal sky, and he could
slip through and find his master.

On the morning of the day when the Grand
Leddy came Bobby watched the holiday crowd
gather on Heriot's Hospital grounds. The
mothers and sisters of hundreds of boys were
there, looking on at the great match game of
cricket. Bobby dropped over the wall and
scampered about, taking a merry part in the
play. When the pupils' procession was formed,
and the long line of grinning and nudging laddies
marched in to service in the chapel and dinner
in the hall, he was set up over the kirkyard wall,
hundreds of hands were waved to him, and
voices called back: "Fareweel, Bobby!" Then

the time-gun boomed from the Castle, and the
little dog trotted up for his dinner and nap under
the settle and his daily visit with Mr. Traill.

In fair weather, when the last guest had departed and the music bells of St.Giles had ceased
playing, the landlord was fond of standing in his
doorway, bareheaded and in shirt-sleeves and
apron, to exchange opinions on politics, litera-
ture and religion, or to tell Bobby's story to
what passers-by he could beguile into talk. At
his feet, there, was a fine place for a sociable little
dog to spend an hour. When he was ready to
go Bobby set his paws upon Mr. Traill and waited
for the landlord's hand to be laid on his head and
the man to say, in the dialect the little dog best
understood: "Bide a wee. Ye're no' needin' to
gang sae sune, laddie!"

At that he dropped, barked politely, wagged
his tail, and was off. If Mr. Traill really wanted
to detain Bobby he had only to withhold the
magic word "laddie," that no one else had used
toward the little dog since Auld Jock died. But
if the word was too long in coming, Bobby would
thrash his tail about impatiently, look up appeal-
ingly, and finally rise and beg and whimper.

"Weel, then, bide wi' me, an' ye'll get it ilka
hour o' the day, ye sonsie, wee, takin' bit! What
are ye hangin' aroond for? Eh—weel—gang

awa' wi' ye—laddie!'' The landlord sighed and looked down reproachfully. With a delighted yelp, and a lick of the lingering hand, Bobby was off.

It was after three o'clock on this day when he returned to the kirkyard. The caretaker was working at the upper end, and the little dog was lonely. But, long enough absent from his master, Bobby lay down on the grave, in the stillness of the mid-afternoon. The robin made a brief call and, as no other birds were about, hopped upon Bobby's back, perched on his head, and warbled a little song. It was then that the gate clicked. Dismissing her carriage and telling the coachman to return at five, Lady Burdett-Coutts entered the kirkyard.

Bobby trotted around the kirk on the chance of meeting a friend. He looked up intently at the strange lady for a moment, and she stood still and looked down at him. She was not a beautiful lady, nor very young. Indeed, she was a few years older than the Queen, and the Queen was a widowed grandmother. But she had a sweet dignity and warm serenity—an unhurried look, as if she had all the time in the world for a wee dog; and Bobby was an age-whitened muff of a plaintive terrier that captured her heart at once. Very certain that this stranger knew and cared about how he felt, Bobby turned and led her down to Auld Jock's grave. And when she was seated on the table-tomb he came up to her and let her look at his collar, and he stood under her caress, although she spoke to him in fey English, calling him a darling little dog. Then, entirely contented with her company, he lay down, his eyes fixed upon her and lolling his tongue.

The sun was on the green and flowery slope of Greyfriars, warming the weathered tombs and the rear windows of the tenements. The Grand Leddy found a great deal there to interest her beside Bobby and the robin that chirped and picked up crumbs between the little dog's paws. Presently the gate was opened again and a housemaid from some mansion in George Square came around the kirk. Trained by Mistress Jeanie, she was a neat and pretty and pleasant-mannered housemaid, in a black gown and white apron, and with a frilled cap on her crinkly, gold-brown hair that had had more than "a lick or twa the nicht afore."

"It's juist Ailie," Bobby seemed to say, as he stood a moment with crested neck and tail. "Ilka body kens Ailie."

The servant lassie, with an hour out, had stopped to speak to Bobby She had not meant to stay long, but the lady, who didn't look in the least grand, began to think friendly things aloud.

"The windows of the tenements are very clean."

"Ay. The bairnies couldna see Bobby gin the windows warna washed." The lassie was pulling her adored little pet's ears, and Bobby was nuzzling up to her.

"In many of the windows there is a box of flowers, or of kitchen herbs to make the broth savory."

"It wasna so i' the auld days. It was aye washin's clappin' aboon the stanes. Noo, mony o' the mithers hang the claes oot at nicht. Ilka thing is changed sin' I was a wean an' leevin' i' the auld Guildhall, the bairnies haen Bobby to lo'e, an' no' to be neglectet." She continued the conversation to include Tammy as he came around the kirk on his tapping crutches.

"Hoo mony years is it, Tammy, sin' Bobby's been leevin' i' the auld kirkyaird? At Maister Traill's snawy picnic ye war five gangin' on sax." They exchanged glances in which lay one of the happy memories of sad childhoods.

"Noo I'm nineteen going on twenty. It's near fourteen years syne, Ailie." Nearly all the burrs had been pulled from Tammy's tongue, but he used a Scotch word now and then, no' to shame Ailie's less cultivated speech.

"So long?" murmured the Grand Leddy. "Bobby is getting old, very old for a terrier."

As if to deny that, Bobby suddenly shot down the slope in answer to a cry of alarm from a song thrush. Still good for a dash, when he came back he dropped panting. The lady put her hand on his rippling coat and felt his heart pounding. Then she looked at his worn-down teeth and lifted his veil. Much of the luster was gone from Bobby's brown eyes, but they were still soft and deep and appealing.

From the windows children looked down upon the quiet group and, without in the least knowing why they wanted to be there, too, the tenement bairns began to drop into the kirkyard. Almost at once it rained—a quick, bright, dashing shower that sent them all flying and laughing up to the shelter of the portico to the new kirk. Bobby scampered up, too, and with the bairns in holiday duddies crowding about her, and the wee dog lolling at her feet, the Grand Leddy talked fairy stories.

She told them all about a pretty country place near London. It was called Holly Lodge because its hedges were bright with green leaves and red berries, even in winter. A lady who had no family at all lived there, and to keep her company she had all sorts of pets. Peter and Prince were the dearest dogs, and Cocky was a parrot that could say the most amusing things. Sir Garnet was the llama goat, or sheep—she didn't know which. There was a fat and lazy old pony that had long been pensioned off on oats and clover, and—oh yes—the white donkey must not be forgotten!

"O-o-o-oh! I didna ken there wad be ony white donkeys!" cried a big-eyed laddie.

"There cannot be many, and there's a story about how the lady came to have this one. One day, driving in a poor street, she saw a coster— that is a London peddler—beating his tired donkey that refused to pull the load. The lady got out of her carriage, fed the animal some carrots from the cart, talked kindly to him right into his big, surprised ear, and stroked his nose. Presently the poor beast felt better and started off cheerfully with the heavy cart. When many costers learned that it was not only wicked but foolish to abuse their patient animals, they hunted for a white donkey to give the lady. They put a collar of flowers about his neck, and brought him up on a platform before a crowd of people. Everybody laughed, for he was a clumsy and comical beast to be decorated with roses and daisies. But the lady is proud of him, and now that pampered donkey has nothing to do but pull her Bath chair about, when she is at Holly Lodge, and kick up his heels on a clover pasture."

"Are ye kennin' anither tale, Leddy?"

"Oh, a number of them. Prince, the fox terrier, was ill once, and the doctor who came to see him said his mistress gave him too much to eat. That was very probable, because that lady likes to see children and animals have too much to eat. There are dozens and dozens of poor children that the lady knows and loves. Once they lived in a very dark and dirty and crowded tenement, quite as bad as some that were torn down in the Cowgate and the Grass-market."

"It mak's ye fecht ane anither," said one laddie, soberly. "Gin they had a sonsie doggie like Bobby to lo'e, an' an auld kirkyaird wi' posies an' birdies to leuk into, they wadna fecht sae muckle."

"I'm very sure of that. Well, the lady built a new tenement with plenty of room and light and air, and a market so they can get better food more cheaply, and a large church, that is also a kind of school where big and little people can learn many things. She gives the children of the neighborhood a Christmas dinner and a gay tree, and she strips the hedges of Holly Lodge for them, and then she takes Peter and Prince and Cocky the parrot, to help along the fun, and she tells her newest stories. Next Christmas she means to tell the story of Greyfriars Bobby, and how all his little Scotch friends are better-behaving and cleaner and happier because they have that wee dog to love."

"Ilka body lo'es Bobby. He wasna ever mistreatet or neglectet," said Ailie, thoughtfully.

"Oh—my—dear! That's the very best part of the story!" The Grand Leddy had a shining look.

The rain had ceased and the sun come out, and the children began to be called away. There was quite a little ceremony of lingering leave-taking with the lady and with Bobby, and while this was going on Ailie had a "sairious" confidence for her old playfellow.

"Tammy, as the leddy says, Bobby's gettin' auld. I ken whaur's a snawy hawthorn aboon the burn in Swanston Dell. The throstles nest there, an' the blackbirds whustle bonny. It isna so far but the bairnies could march oot wi' posies." She turned to the lady, who had overheard her. "We gied a promise to the Laird Provost to gie Bobby a grand funeral. Ye ken he wullna be permittet to be buried i' the kirkyaird."

"Will he not? I had not thought of that."

Her tone was at once hushed and startled
Then she was down in the grass, brooding over
the little dog, and Bobby had the pathetic look
of trying to understand what this emotional talk,
that seemed to concern himself, was about.
Tammy and Ailie were down, too.

"Are ye thinkin' Bobby wull be kennin' the
deeference?" Ailie's bluebell eyes were wide at
the thought of pain for this little pet.

"I do not know, my dear. But there cannot
well be more love in this world than there is
room for in God's heaven."

She was silent all the way to the gate, some
thought in her mind already working toward a
gracious deed. At the last she said: "The little
dog is fond of you both. Be with him all you
can, for I think his beautiful life is near its end."
After a pause, during which her face was lighted
by a smile, as if from a lovely thought within,
she added: "Don't let Bobby die before my
return from London."

In a week she was back, and in the meantime
letters and telegrams had been flying, and many
wheels set in motion in wee Bobby's affairs.
When she returned to the churchyard, very early
one morning, no less a person than the Lord
Provost himself was with her. Five years had
passed, but Mr. — no, Sir William — Chambers,

GREYFRIARS BOBBY

Laird of Glenormiston, for he had been knighted by the Queen, was still Lord Provost of Edinburgh.

Almost immediately Mr. Traill appeared, by appointment, and was made all but speechless for once in his loquacious life by the honor of being asked to tell Bobby's story to the Baroness Burdett-Coutts. But not even a tenement child or a London coster could be ill at ease with the Grand Leddy for very long, and presently the three were in close conference in the portico. Bobby welcomed them, and then dozed in the sun and visited with the robin on Auld Jock's grave. Far from being tongue-tied, the landlord was inspired. What did he not remember, from the pathetic renunciation, "Bobby isna ma ain dog," down to the leal Highlander's last, near-tragic reminder to men that in the nameless grave lay his unforgotten master.

He sketched the scene in Haddo's Hole, where the tenement bairns poured out as pure a gift of love and mercy and self-sacrifice as had ever been laid at the foot of a Scottish altar. He told of the search for the lately ransomed and lost terrier, by the lavish use of oil and candles; of Bobby's coming down Castle Rock in the fog, battered and bruised for a month's careful tending by an old Heriot laddie. His feet still showed the scars of that perilous descent. He himself, remorseful, had gone with the Bible-reader from the Medical Mission in the Cowgate to the dormer-lighted closet in College Wynd, where Auld Jock had died. Now he described the classic fireplace of white freestone, with its boxed-in bed, where the Pentland shepherd lay like some effigy on a bier, with the wee guardian dog stretched on the flagged hearth below.

"What a subject for a monument!" The Grand Leddy looked across the top of the slope at the sleeping Skye. "I suppose there is no portrait of Bobby."

"Ay, your Leddyship; I have a drawing in the dining-rooms, sketched by Mr. Daniel Maclise. He was here a year or twa ago, just before his death, doing some commission, and often had his tea in my bit place. I told him Bobby's story, and he made the sketch for me as a souvenir of his veesit."

"I am sure you prize it, Mr. Traill. Mr. Maclise was a talented artist, but he was not especially an animal painter. There really is no one since Landseer paints no more."

"I would advise you, Baroness, not to make that remark at an Edinburgh dinner-table." Glenormiston was smiling. "The pride of Auld Reekie just now is Mr. Gourlay Stelle, who was lately commanded to Balmoral Castle to paint the Queen's dogs."

"The very person! I have seen his beautiful canvas—'Burns and the Field Mouse.' Is he not a younger brother of Sir John Stelle, the sculptor of the statue and character figures in the Scott monument?" Her eyes sparkled as she added: "You have so much talent of the right sorts here that it would be wicked not to employ it in the good cause."

What "the good cause" was came out presently, in the church, where she startled even Glenormiston and Mr. Traill by saying quietly to the minister and the church officers of Greyfriars auld kirk: "When Bobby dies I want him laid in the grave with his master."

Every member of both congregations knew Bobby and was proud of his fame, but no official notice had ever been taken of the little dog's presence in the churchyard. The elders and deacons were, in truth, surprised that such distinguished attention should be directed to him now, and they were embarrassed by it. It was not easy for any body of men in the United Kingdom to refuse anything to Lady Burdett-Coutts, because she could always count upon having the sympathy of the public. But this, they declared, could not be considered.

GREYFRIARS BOBBY

To propose to bury a dog in the historic church-yard would scandalize the city. To this objection Glenormiston said, seriously: "The feeling about Bobby is quite exceptional. I would be willing to put the matter to the test of heading a petition."

At that the church officers threw up their hands. They preferred to sound public sentiment themselves, and would consider it. But if Bobby was permitted to be buried with his master there must be no notice taken of it. Well, the Heriot laddies might line up along the wall, and the tenement bairns look down from the windows. Would that satisfy her ladyship?

"As far as it goes." The Grand Leddy was smiling, but a little tremulous about the mouth.

That was a day when women had little to say in public, and she meant to make a speech, and to ask to be allowed to do an unheard-of thing.

"I want to put up a monument to the nameless man who inspired such love, and to the little dog that was capable of giving it. Ah! gentlemen, do not refuse, now." She sketched her idea of the classic fireplace bier, the dead shepherd of the Pentlands, and the little prostrate terrier. "Immemorial man and his faithful dog. Our society for the prevention of cruelty to animals is finding it so hard to get

280

people even to admit the sacredness of life in dumb creatures, the brutalizing effects of abuse of them on human beings, and the moral and practical worth to us of kindness. To insist that a dog feels, that he loves devotedly and with less calculation than men, that he grieves at a master's death and remembers him long years, brings a smile of amusement. Ah yes! Here in Scotland, too, where your own great Lord Erskine was a pioneer of pity two generations ago, and with Sir Walter's dogs beloved of the literary, and Doctor Brown's immortal 'Rab,' we find it up-hill work.

"The story of Greyfriars Bobby is quite the most complete and remarkable ever recorded in dog annals. His lifetime of devotion has been witnessed by thousands, and honored publicly, by your own Lord Provost, with the freedom of the city, a thing that, I believe, has no precedent. All the endearing qualities of the dog reach their height in this loyal and lovable Highland ter-rier; and he seems to have brought out the best qualities of the people who have known him. Indeed, for fourteen years hundreds of disin-herited children have been made kinder and happier by knowing Bobby's story and having that little dog to love."

She stopped in some embarrassment, seeing

how she had let herself go, in this warm champ
pionship, and then she added: "Bobby does not
need a monument, but I think we need one of
him, that future generations may never forget
what the love of a dog may mean, to himself and
to us."

The Grand Leddy must have won her plea,
then and there, but for the fact that the matter
of erecting a monument of a public character
anywhere in the city had to come up before the
Burgh council. In that body the stubborn op-
position of a few members unexpectedly devel-
oped, and, in spite of popular sympathy with the
proposal, the plan was rejected. Permission
was given, however, for Lady Burdett-Coutts to
put up a suitable memorial to Bobby at the end
of George IV. Bridge, and opposite the main
gateway to the kirkyard.

For such a public place a tomb was unsuitable.
What form the memorial was to take was not
decided upon until, because of two chance hap-
penings of one morning, the form of it bloomed
like a flower in the soul of the Grand Leddy.
She had come down to the kirkyard to watch the
artist at work. Morning after morning he had
sketched there. He had drawn Bobby lying
down, his nose on his paws, asleep on the grave.
He had drawn him sitting upon the table-tomb,

and standing in the begging attitude in which
he was so irresistible. But with every sketch
he was dissatisfied.

Bobby was a trying and deceptive subject.
He had the air of curiosity and gaiety of other
terriers. He saw no sense at all in keeping still,
with his muzzle tipped up or down, and his tail
held just so. He brushed all that unreasonable
man's suggestions aside as quite unworthy of
consideration. Besides, he had the liveliest
interest in the astonishing little dog that grew
and disappeared, and came back, in some new
attitude, on the canvas. He scraped acquaintance with it once or twice to the damage of
fresh brush-work. He was always jumping from
his pose and running around the easel to see how
the latest dog was coming on.

After a number of mornings Bobby lost interest
in the man and his occupation and went about
his ordinary routine of life as if the artist was
not there at all. One morning the wee terrier
was found sitting on the table-tomb, on his
haunches, looking up toward the Castle, where
clouds and birds were blown around the sun-
gilded battlements.

His attitude might have meant anything or
nothing, for the man who looked at him from
above could not see his expression. And all at

once he realized that to see Bobby a human being must get down to his level. To the scandal of the children, he lay on his back on the grass and did nothing at all but look up at Bobby until the little dog moved. Then he set the wee Highlander up on an altar-topped shaft just above the level of the human eye. Indifferent at the moment as to what was done to him, Bobby continued to gaze up and out, wistfully and patiently, upon this masterless world. As plainly as a little dog could speak, Bobby said:

"I hae bided lang an' lanely. Hoo lang hae I still to bide? An' syne, wull I be gangin' to Auld Jock?"

The Grand Leddy saw that at once, and tears started to her eyes when she came in to find the artist sketching with feverish rapidity. She confessed that she had looked into Bobby's eyes, but she had never truly seen that mourning little creature before. He had only to be set up so, in bronze, and looking through the kirkyard gate, to tell his own story to the most careless passer-by. The image of the simple memorial was clear in her mind, and it seemed unlikely that anything could be added to it, when she left the kirkyard.

As she was getting into her carriage a noble collie, but one with a discouraged tail and hanging tongue, came out of Forest Road. He had done a hard morning's work, of driving a flock from the Pentlands to the cattle and sheep market, and then had hunted far and unsuccessfully for water. He nosed along the gutter, here and there licking from the cobblestones what muddy moisture had not drained away from a recent rain. The same lady who had fed the carrots to the coster's donkey in London turned hastily into Ye Olde Greyfriars Dining-Rooms, and asked Mr. Traill for a basin of water. The landlord thought he must have misunderstood her.

"Is it a glass of water your Leddyship's wanting?"

"No, a basin, please! a large one, and very quickly."

She took it from him, hurried out, and set it under the thirsty animal's nose. The collie lapped it eagerly until the water was gone, then looked up and, by waggings and lickings, asked for more. Mr. Traill brought out a second basin, and he remarked upon a sheep-dog's capacity for water.

"It's no' a basin will satisfy him, used as he is to having a tarn on the moor to drink from. This neeborhood is noted for the dogs that are aye passing. On Wednesdays the farm dogs come up from the Grassmarket, and every day, there are weel-cared-for dogs from the residence streets, dogs of all conditions across the bridge from High Street, and meeserable waifs from the Cowgate. Stray pussies are about, too. I'm a gude-hearted man, and an unco' observant one, your Leddyship, but I was no' thinking that these animals must often suffer from thirst."

"Few people do think of it. Most men can love some one dog or cat or horse and be attentive to its wants, but they take little thought for the world of dumb animals that are so dependent upon us. It is no special credit to you, Mr. Traill, that you became fond of an attractive little dog like Bobby and have cared for him so tenderly."

The landlord gasped. He had taken not a little pride in his stanch championship and watchful care of Bobby, and his pride had been increased by the admiration that had been lavished on him for years by the general public. Now, as he afterward confessed to Mr. Brown:

"Her leddyship made me feel I'd done nae-thing by the ordinar', but maistly to please my ainsel'. Eh, man, she made me sing sma'."

When the collie had finished drinking, he looked up gratefully, rubbed against the good Samaritans, waved his plumed tail like a banner,

and trotted away.   After a thoughtful moment
Lady Burdett-Coutts said:

"The suitable memorial here, Mr. Traill, is a
fountain, with a low basin level with the curb,
and a higher one, and Bobby sitting on an altar-
topped central column above, looking through
the kirkyard gate.   It shall be his mission to
bring men and small animals together in sympathy by offering to both the cup of cold water."

She was there once again that year.   On her
way north she stopped in Edinburgh over night
to see how the work on the fountain had pro-
gressed.   It was in Scotland's best season, most
of the days dry and bright and sharp.   But on
that day it was misting, and yellow leaves were
dropping on the wet tombs and beaded grass,
when the Grand Leddy appeared at the kirkyard
late in the afternoon with a wreath of laurel to
lay on Auld Jock's grave.

Bobby slipped out, dry as his own delectable
bone, from under the tomb of Mistress Jean
Grant, and nearly wagged his tail off with pleasure.   Mistress Jeanie was set in a proud flutter
when the Grand Leddy rang at the lodge kitchen
and asked if she and Bobby could have their tea
there with the old couple by the cozy grate fire.

They all drank tea from the best blue cups,
and ate buttered scones and strawberry jam on

the scoured deal table. Bobby had his porridge
and broth on the hearth. The coals snapped in
the grate and the firelight danced merrily on the
skylark's cage and the copper kettle. Mr. Brown
got out his fife and played "Bonnie Dundee."
Wee, silver-white Bobby tried to dance, but he
tumbled over so lamentably once or twice that
he hung his head apologetically, admitting that
he ought to have the sense to know that his
dancing days were done. He lay down and
lolled and blinked on the hearth until the Grand
Leddy rose to go.

"I am on my way to Braemar to visit for a few
days at Balmoral Castle. I wish I could take
Bobby with me to show him to the dear Queen."

"Preserve me!" cried Mistress Jeanie, and Mr.
Brown's pet pipe was in fragments on the hearth.

Bobby leaped upon her and whimpered, saying "Dinna gang, Leddy!" as plainly as a little
dog could say anything. He showed the pathos
at parting with one he was fond of, now, that an
old and affectionate person shows. He clung to
her gown, rubbed his rough head under her
hand, and trotted disconsolately beside her to
her waiting carriage. At the very last she said,
sadly:

"The Queen will have to come to Edinburgh to
see Bobby."

GREYFRIARS BOBBY

"The bonny wee wad be a prood doggie, yer Leddyship," Mistress Jeanie managed to stammer, but Mr. Brown was beyond speech.

The Grand Leddy said nothing. She looked at the foundation work of Bobby's memorial fountain, swathed in canvas against the winter, and waiting—waiting for the spring, when the waters of the earth should be unsealed again; waiting until finis could be written to a story on a bronze tablet; waiting for the effigy of a shaggy Skye terrier to be cast and set up; waiting—

When the Queen came to see Bobby it was unlikely that he would know anything about it.

He would know nothing of the crowds to gather there on a public occasion, massing on the bridge, in Greyfriars Place, in broad Chambers Street, and down Candlemakers Row—the magistrates and Burgh council, professors and students from the University, soldiers from the Castle, the neighboring nobility in carriages, farmers and shepherds from the Pentlands, the Heriot laddies marching from the school, and the tenement children in holiday duddies—all to honor the memory of a devoted little dog. He would know nothing of the military music and flowers, the prayer of the minister of Greyfriars auld kirk, the speech of the Lord Provost; nothing of the happy tears of the Grand Leddy when a veil should fall

away from a little bronze dog that gazed wistfully through the kirkyard gate, and water gush
forth for the refreshment of men and animals.

"Good-by, good-by, good-by, Bobby; most
loving and lovable, darlingest wee dog in the
world!" she cried, and a shower of bright drops
and sweet little sounds fell on Bobby's tousled
head. Then the carriage of the Grand Leddy
rolled away in the rainy dusk.

The hour-bell of St. Giles was rung, and the
sunset bugle blown in the Castle. It took Mr.
Brown a long time to lift the wicket, close the tall
leaves and lock the gate. The wind was rising,
and the air hardening. One after one the gas-
lamps flared in the gusts that blew on the bridge.
The huge bulk of shadow lay, velvet black, in the
drenched quarry pit of the Grassmarket. The
caretaker's voice was husky with a sudden " cauld
in 'is heid."

"Ye're an auld dog, Bobby, an' ye canna deny
it. Ye'll juist hae to sleep i' the hoose the
misty nicht."

Loath to part with them, Bobby went up to
the lodge with the old couple and saw them
within the cheerful kitchen. But when the door
was held open for him, he wagged his tail in farewell and trotted away around the kirk. All the
concession he was willing to make to old age and

bad weather was to sleep under the fallen table tomb.

Greyfriars on a dripping autumn evening! A pensive hour and season, everything memorable brooded there. Crouched back in shadowy ranks, the old tombs were draped in mystery. The mist was swirled by the wind and smoke smeared out, over their dim shapes. Where families sat close about scant suppers, the lights of candles and cruisey lamps were blurred. The faintest halo hung above the Castle head. Infrequent footsteps hurried by the gate. There was the rattle of a belated cart, the ring of a distant church bell. But even on such nights the casements were opened and little faces looked into the melancholy kirkyard. Candles glimmered for a moment on the murk, and sweetly and clearly the tenement bairns called down:

"A gude nicht to ye, Bobby."

They could not see the little dog, but they knew he was there. They knew now that he would still be there when they could see him no more—his body a part of the soil, his memory a part of all that was held dear and imperishable in that old garden of souls. They could go up to the lodge and look at his famous collar, and they would have his image in bronze on the fountain. And sometime, when the mysterious door opened for them, they might see Bobby again, a sonsie doggie running on the green pastures and beside the still waters, at the heels of his shepherd master, for:

If there is not more love in this world than there is room for in God's heaven, Bobby would 'ust have " gaen awa' hame."